TODD SMITH

IGNITING
REVIVAL FIRE
EVERY DAY

70 Invitations that Awaken Your Heart
from Global Revivalists including:

SID ROTH

BILL JOHNSON

RANDY CLARK

ROBERTS LIARDON

JOHN KILPATRICK

DAVID HOGAN

JAMES W. GOLL

PAT & KAREN SCHATZLINE

JOHN & CAROL ARN

DR. MICHAEL BRO

and more!

D1512294

DESTINY IMAGE® PUBLISHERS, INC.

P.O. Box 310, Shippensburg, PA 17257-0310

"Promoting Inspired Lives."

This book and all other Destiny Image and Destiny Image Fiction books are available at Christian bookstores and distributors worldwide.

Cover design by: Eileen Rockwell

Interior design by Terry Clifton

For more information on foreign distributors, call 717-532-3040.

Reach us on the Internet: www.destinyimage.com.

ISBN 13 TP: 978-0-7684-5710-0

ISBN 13 eBook: 978-0-7684-5711-7

ISBN 13 HC: 978-0-7684-5713-1

ISBN 13 LP: 978-0-7684-5712-4

For Worldwide Distribution, Printed in the U.S.A.

1 2 3 4 5 6 7 8 / 24 23 22 21 20

Contents

1

There Is More!

THE WORDS ARE SIMPLE AND THE SENTENCE IS SHORT. JUST three words total, eleven letters in all. *There...is...more.* That's it! And yet these three words articulate the cry of many a Christian's heart. Deep down, we know there is more.

And it's not because we are malcontents or grumblers, or because we can never be satisfied. Instead, as we walk with the Lord, as we encounter His Spirit, as we look at Jesus, as we meditate on Scripture, from the depths of our heart a cry rises to Heaven, "Lord, there must be more!"

Speaking personally, God has not appointed me to be the judge of His Church. He has not called me to be a holy policeman or an accuser of the brethren. My goal is to build up, not tear down, and I thank God for everything He is doing in every church in the country, be it a house church or a megachurch. But I cannot deny that something is missing. I cannot deny that there is more. If your heart affirms these words, that is a healthy sign.

Simply stated, if the Bible is true (which it is) and if Jesus really rose from the dead and sent the Spirit (which He did), then *there must be more.* There has to be more. Every page of the New Testament shouts to us that there is more. Why not be honest and say it out loud: "God, I know there is more!"

To say that something is missing is to glorify the Lord. To say that something is not lining up is to be honest before Heaven. To say that what you read in the Word is different from what you experience in life is to honor the testimony of Jesus.

He shed His blood so we could be transformed. So we could overcome the enemy. So we could be His Spirit-filled ambassadors. So we could set the captives free and heal the wounded and dying. There is so much more He still wants to do through you and through me.

He *longs* to manifest His grace in us and through us. He *longs* to reveal Himself to us. He *longs* to pour out His Spirit in power. He is more ready to bless and to fill and to ignite and to anoint than we are to receive.

But are we ready? Are we hungry? Are we desperate? Do our prayers bleed? Do we have room for more of God's presence and power and purpose—in our hearts, in our homes, in our congregations?

Look carefully at the words of Jesus to the churches in Revelation.

To Sardis He said, "I know your deeds; you have a reputation of being alive, but you are dead" (Rev. 3:1 NIV). They looked good on the outside, but inwardly they were dead.

His word to Laodicea were even stronger: "You say, 'I am rich; I have acquired wealth and do not need a thing.' But you do not realize that you are wretched, pitiful, poor, blind and naked" (Rev. 3:17 NIV).

They were the happening church, the prosperous church, the successful church—at least, in their own eyes—but in reality they were pitiful, poor, and blind.

There's a message here for us! When we are self-satisfied and proud, we will not be desperate for God. We will be filled with ourselves, with our programs and our meetings and our budgets and our activities and self-congratulations. We have arrived! We have achieved our goals! Look at us!

There is no room for the Spirit's moving in a place like that, no room for visitation, no room for revival. Like Laodicea we boast of our wealth (be it spiritual or material); like Sardis we think we are alive.

But God sees the condition of our souls—how we have exchanged professionalism for the anointing, how we have traded dependence on the Spirit for fleshly endeavors, how we have substituted a carnal business approach for our first love devotion. Now is the time to awaken!

What is the condition of *your* heart today? Are you hungry, thirsty, and desperate? That is an excellent sign. Self-satisfaction is a spiritual curse.

There is more!

Dr. Michael Brown
Author, professor
Radio host, *Ask Dr. Brown*

2

Revival: The Word Fulfilled

The kingdom of heaven suffers violence,
and the violent take it by force.
—MATTHEW 11:12

CHARLES FINNEY ONCE SAID, "REVIVAL IS NO MORE A MIRA-cle than a crop of wheat. Revival comes from Heaven when heroic souls enter the conflict determined to win or die—or if need be, to win and die."

Among other things, revival is a product of the Word of God taking root in a person's life. We know, according to Romans 10:17, that faith springs up in our hearts as we hear it and meditate on it. In Joshua 1:8, the Lord instructs Joshua to meditate on the Word that he might do the Word he meditates. James tells us that it is the doer of the Word who is blessed, not the hearer only (see James 1:25).

The admonishment of Scripture is that we take hold of the Word of God and not be shaken easily from the promise of God. Paul told Timothy to "Fight the good fight of faith, lay hold on eternal life" (1 Tim. 6:12). One Greek lexicon explains this to mean that we should *grab a double handful*. Like a man trying to ride a wild stallion without a saddle, he would wrap his fingers in the mane and hold on. We are to grab hold of the words of life and take possession of every promise given to us.

When the false prophets and false dreamers of Jeremiah's day were misleading the people and causing them to forget God and His Word, God intervened by reminding them of the power of His Word.

> *Is not my word like as a fire? saith the Lord; and*
> *like a hammer that breaketh the rock in pieces?*
> (Jeremiah 23:29 KJV)

The Word of God can burn up and demolish any obstruction that would stand in the way of its fulfillment in your life. No mountain is so big that it can withstand the voice that speaks through the spirit of faith. A mighty boulder can be removed by the constant chipping away of a persistent hammer. Revival will manifest as we take the hammer of God's Word and consistently strike the hard obstacles in our way. We will see the desired change as we allow the fire of God's Word to burn the impurities of sin and neglect of holy things out of our lives and are permeated with the sacred fire of God.

As we patiently await the manifestation of the promised Word, we watch for the sprouting of a seed. Jesus taught us that His Word is a seed that produces thirty, sixty, and a hundredfold when properly stewarded in the hearts and lives of His followers. Often, the seed (Word) begins to sprout. It seems small and insignificant. It appears without fanfare. The sprouting seed looks nothing like the mighty oak. In our desperation and zeal for the prophetic promises of God to come to pass, we often miss the sprouting seed because it looks nothing like the image we've conjured in our minds. Isaiah warned Israel not to miss the coming Messiah when he penned these words:

> For he shall grow up before him as a tender plant, and as a root out of dry ground: he hath no form nor comeliness; and when we see him, there is no beauty that we should desire him (Isaiah 53:2 KJV).

Isaiah got a glimpse of this promised Seed. The religious leaders and people of Jesus' day saw this Seed in the flesh. Yet all of their education failed when they could not recognize the value of the Seed standing among them. The greatest promise God ever made began its fulfillment as a seed; why would He change His mode of operation in our day? As we contend for revival in our families, communities, and the nations, we must remember to place a high value on the seed—the Word promised to us.

In light of Finney's statement concerning revival, any promise from God must be given our utmost attention (lay hold on it) and dedication (steward the seed). One must be determined to hold on to the promise, no matter the circumstances. "Let us labour therefore to enter into that rest" (Heb. 4:11 KJV).

PASTORS JASON and MANDY ADAIR
Victorious Faith Church
www.JasonAdairMinistries.com

3

Check Your Oil

*And the foolish said to the wise, "Give us some
of your oil, for our lamps are going out." But the
wise answered, saying, "No, lest there should
not be enough for us and you; but go rather
to those who sell, and buy for yourselves."*

—Matthew 25:8-9

"Awake, Church! What was set ablaze by the agonizing of our forefathers cannot forever keep our own lamps lit." As I read these words penned by the late evangelist Steve Hill, something shot through my soul. I've spent my entire life as a student of historic revival. There is such a deep well to be drawn from the lives of those who have gone before us.

Their lamps were lit in the secret place—set ablaze by holiness and consecration, tears shed in prayer and intercession. They were not spurred on by the lights of a stage or the cheers of the crowd. They did not "psych themselves up" to perform, but instead got low on their faces so they could come before the King of kings. These were men and women of God who carried a vast reserve of the things of God. They were prepared to tarry as long as it took for the bridegroom to come.

However, much like the parable referenced above, there has risen a generation of "foolish virgins" who indeed have a lamp, but have not paid the price to purchase their own reserve of oil. They are filled with just enough to shine for a few moments when their services are called upon. They have gotten on for some time in this way and have fallen more in love with performing at weddings than tarrying for the bridegroom. Over time, they have become comfortable in the fact that nothing more has been required of them. Just before the spotlight is on, it has become all too easy to quickly reach for a drop of Finney's oil, or perhaps a bit of Spurgeon's or Wesley's oil will contain something thought-provoking. With the intent to repackage this ancient oil and brand it as their own, they call out to these wise virgins who have gone before, "Give us some of your oil!" As I write this very article in the study of the late Leonard Ravenhill, I can almost hear their response: "You must buy your own!"

Is it any surprise that much ministry today more closely resembles that of Simon the Sorcerer than the apostle Paul? Large crowds are gathered, and men are impressed by tricks and displays of human greatness instead of being transformed by the message born of a prophet, impregnated in the secret place through intimacy with God. Could it be because their performance has been born of the same heart? This precious oil cannot be purchased with money, nor can it be obtained through an instantaneous experience in a prayer line. While we have all had powerful encounters through the laying on of hands, and this is biblical, I believe these types of impartations only increase the capacity of our vessels. Indeed, we must still fill them with precious oil.

This oil can be purchased in one place and one place only. It is the purchase spoken of in Revelation 3:18. This purchase will leave us with riches in abundance to pour into the Body of Christ, with true holiness, and with eyes that see clearly. It can be purchased only in the place of intimacy with God!

Like these poor, foolish virgins, shall we be caught unprepared when the long-awaited moment finally comes? Shall we spend our entire lives crying out for revival and, when the midnight cry goes forth and the Church is awakened, be found unprepared? One day it will be too late to buy oil—in fact, in the parable, it was while they were out purchasing oil that the bridegroom came. We must respond urgently! We must prepare ourselves while there is still time! Perhaps the greatest awakening in the history of the Church is ahead of us, and we do not want to be out of place when He comes. How would you have Him find you at His coming?

EVANGELIST LEVI LUTZ
Together in the Harvest
Togetherintheharvest.com

4

How to Get Spiritual Hunger

You will seek Me and find Me, when you
search for Me with all your heart.
—JEREMIAH 29:13

IF YOU WISH YOU HAD SPIRITUAL HUNGER, BUT DULLNESS numbs you or problems overwhelm you, the good news is you can do something about it. Whether you've never had a truly personal relationship with your Creator God, or whether you've somehow moved away from Him, the solution is the same.

Ask. Just ask. And keep on asking. The One who is the Author and Finisher of your faith will always answer. Each asking is a seed planted that will in time bear fruit, just like an ear of corn. The natural world illustrates the spiritual. Corn germinates in weeks and matures in around three months. So keep asking for at least that long. "God, if You're there, make me hungry for You."

In a short time, like a bright green shoot poking forth, you will feel something altogether new—a heart tug to come aside. It is an invitation. If you stop whatever you're doing, shut off the television, close the computer, and come aside, you'll find He is there waiting for you. That's what Moses did when he saw a bush burning, but not charred. He paused and wondered and thereby created parentheses in time into which God spoke.

If feeling your life fire flickering, you have the ear of the One who will not extinguish a smoldering wick. Don't listen to the lie that He's holding out on you. He exchanged the life of His only Son for your life. How much more will He not freely give you all things, especially His presence?

Consider that the very source of your desire for spiritual hunger is actually the Lord Himself, calling to you. Deep calls to deep. Your personal desire may just be part of something much grander that the Lord is stirring up worldwide.

For example, a great tsunami of spiritual hunger swept the entire world in the 1970s. The decade was characterized by thousands experiencing a consuming desire to explore the deep meaning of life itself.

In the US, many came to a relationship with God through Jesus, a movement now called the Jesus Revolution. This was the era of hippies, flower children proclaiming peace and love. Many seekers trekked to remote parts of the world to inquire of truth from gurus. Jews discovered Yeshua (Jesus) as Messiah.

In another example, perhaps little known in the West, hungry prayers drew an outpouring of miraculous healings in central Tallinn, Estonia at the Oleviste Church. From all over the Soviet Union, thousands camped in the train station, then lined up daily for prayer. Discarded crutches dotted the church walls. A deaf-mute was healed, went home, and returned bringing his entire village. A demoniac flew through the air as the power of God hit him and set him free. The Communist opponents were held at bay for a long season by the hand of God.

The cloud of miracles finally lifted. Years later the beleaguered pastor said, "We saw the raw power of the hand of God. Now we seek His face, and seek how to love."

God is love. God is a lover. He loves you and me and has a real desire that His passion be reciprocated. The lover's desire for the beloved is all consuming. Love won't be denied.

Therefore, persistence is the currency for results when asking God for something good. Consider the determination of these Bible characters—friends tore off the roof, lowering their friend before the Healer; the short man climbed a tree; the blind man cried even louder when they shushed him; the outcast woman pushed through the crowd to touch the hem of His garment; the friend kept knocking late at night until he got the bread he wanted; the widow hounded the corrupt judge until he gave her justice.

The Master gave such illustrations to teach that men should always pray and not give up.

"O God, give me spiritual hunger."

Just ask, and keep on asking. He promises to answer.

LESLYE MORGAN SCHNEIER
Beth Hallel
Birmingham, Alabama
www.ShalomBirmingham.com
info@shalombirmingham.com

5

Are You Desperate Enough for Revival?

I AM CONVINCED, NOW MORE THAN EVER, THAT REVIVAL IS the only hope for our nation. It's really revival or else. Our survival as a society is dependent on a revived Church. After all, as the Church goes, so goes the world. We need to seize the moment we have been given. In these days of deep darkness and moral compromise, the Body of Christ cannot afford to remain a sleeping giant. While society as a whole, and even pockets of Christianity, is embracing sin as acceptable, the Church is abandoning the power of Pentecost. The very dynamic that set us apart to begin with is what many have considered unpopular, controversial, and divisive. It's time for us to go after revival with full force. We are not asking God for something new and different; we are longing for a restoration of the old, ancient, and powerful.

What took place on Father's Day, June 18, 1995 *exceeded* my expectations. Yes, He is the God who answers prayers. At the same time, He is also the God of Ephesians 3:20, "who is able to do immeasurably more than all we ask or imagine" (NIV).

When revival hit, I was *not* the most qualified person to pastor such a move of the Holy Spirit. Yes, I attended Bible school, studied church history, and have read several books on the subject of revival. I have taught on revival, preached about revival, and have longed to witness a mighty outpouring of God's Spirit all my life. But what *really* qualifies someone to steward a historic move of the Holy Spirit?

It's certainly not about ability. It's not education. It's not articulation, or eloquence, or even how good a preacher you are. I have simply given my life and ministry to being a custodian of God's presence. That's it. Over the years the Lord has raised me up with this being my driving goal. More than pleasing people, I have endeavored to accommodate God's presence. After all, true, lasting transformation only takes place because of an encounter with the Holy Spirit. Our gimmicks, no matter how great or flashy, don't have what it takes. *God is the only One capable of breaking into a human heart and setting it ablaze with holy zeal.* He alone demolishes strongholds, cancels curses, overcomes impossibilities, breaks addictions, heals sick bodies, and delivers tormented souls.

For many years I prayed a prayer that is surely familiar to many pastors: "Lord, pour out Your Holy Spirit on our church." It's a common prayer, and yet the Lord answered it uncommonly. I still stand in awe that such a prayer was so powerfully answered in my lifetime and before my very eyes during the Brownsville Revival.

The Brownsville Revival was not the result of preaching; it was God's sovereignty colliding with humankind's desperate cry in the place of prayer. In my personal experience, prayer was one of the key factors that paved the way for this extraordinary move of the Holy Spirit. In fact, prayer was a catalyst in pushing me out of my comfort zone and positioning me to be in sync with God's purposes for revival.

In order to accommodate revival, we need to be willing to move beyond the comfortable and familiar. The Holy Spirit wants to move in every single church community in the world. This is a fact. The reason He does not is because many of these communities are unwilling to host Him and cater to His preferences. My decision to integrate Sunday night prayer meetings into the culture at Brownsville was monumental in preparing us for revival. This was not a John Kilpatrick decision; it was a Holy Spirit directive. He told me, "If you will return to the God of your childhood—if you will make this a house of prayer—I will pour out My Spirit here." Without His instruction, I might have continued on, stuck in the same old rut, doing what we always did and seeing what we always saw.

The truth is, *there is no quick and easy way to revival.* We are not going to have true, lasting revival without prayer. Not casual prayer. Not convenient prayer. Not common prayer. *Nothing about revival is birthed in common places. If we desire to see God move in extraordinary ways, we must be willing to do some extraordinary things.*

Paul reminds us that we serve the One who "is able to do far more abundantly beyond all that we ask or think, according to the power that works within us" (Eph. 3:20 NASB).

JOHN KILPATRICK
Lead pastor, Church of His Presence
Daphne, Alabama

6

You Are the Missing Ingredient for Revival!

WE NEED *REVIVAL!* THIS IS A STATEMENT I HAVE HEARD MOST of my life. It seems like the American church has been proclaiming this statement for many years. Even in the midst of many "revivals" or authentic moves of God, Christians continue to demand the need for revival.

My fear is that while crying out for revival we have missed many appointed moments of encounter with God's presence. Oftentimes when God's Spirit begins to move in the midst of His people, we become too pharisaical to realize that God is reviving His Church or us individually.

The Spirit of the Lord told me one time, "Never wrongfully judge the supernatural." Oftentimes when God does something different from what we are used to or comfortable with, we discount it as fleshly. When people react against Holy Spirit manifestations that they are not familiar with, they judge the action as ungodly.

My prayer is, in the midst of our search for times of refreshing revival from the Lord, we do not miss these times by standing on the sidelines refusing to participate because it is unusual. Factually, our God has always manifested Himself in unusual ways. We must embrace what God is doing in the now and not try to design a face for revival that always resembles our past experiences.

C.H. Spurgeon says about revival, "The word *revive* wears its meaning upon its forehead; it is from the Latin, and may be interpreted thus—to live again, to receive again a life which has almost expired; to rekindle into a flame the vital spark which was nearly extinguished."

Revival historian Matthew Backholer, when describing the elements of revival, lists these essential components—revival must exalt Jesus, glorify God, give Holy Spirit His rightful place, revive Christians, save sinners, and call backsliders to repentance.

One thing is for certain. Revival is not about *charisma* but about *character*; therefore, it eliminates every personality except for Christ's! The focus is not on manifestations but on lasting results.

In its infancy, revival has three structural ingredients required. You cannot have revival without *life*, *death*, and a *revivalist*. You can't revive something that was never alive. You can't revive a life that isn't experiencing a realm of death. You can't escape the fact that God always uses someone—a revivalist to bring revival to His people.

Oftentimes in my experiences I have witnessed people looking for the corporate Body of Christ or local churches to initiate revival. However, I believe God's desire is for true revival to begin with us on an individual basis. Corporate revival should always originate from a personal awakening or experience. It was Jesus' personal relationship with the Father that platformed His public ministry. Revival will always be birthed from the privacy of an individual commitment to God and His nature.

I submit to you that you are not waiting for revival but rather revival is waiting for you! I would like to use the story of Jesus meeting the Samaritan woman at a drinking well for a foundation to inspire a truth within you. In John 4 we read how Jesus desired to go through Samaria. Jesus said, "I must go through Samaria," showing how important this meeting was to Him and to the Kingdom of God on earth. Upon His arrival, Jesus didn't find a local church. He didn't wait for a gathering of people to form before He ministered. Rather, the necessary detour to the Samaritan city of Sychar crescendoed with a personal meeting with a sinful woman at a watering well.

Jesus encountered a lady who had five husbands and was in a relationship at the time with a man who was not her husband. She was searching for water that would quench the thirst of her dying soul. She was in need of revival. Jesus met her where she was. He loved her where she was. The moment the woman submitted to His deity and embraced His love for her, she was revived. She was changed from death to life. She was changed from darkness to light. She who was spiritually dead came back to life!

This lady then went into the city and led the multitude back to Jesus. It was the personal revival of an individual that led the city to Jesus! Through time God has always used one man or woman to initiate the miraculous. If God could revive one man or one woman to Himself then He could deliver nations!

I challenge you to stop searching for revival and be revival! You hold the ingredients for revival within yourself. Life, death, and the ability to be a revivalist are all within you. Chase Jesus every day and revival will come!

DAVID EDMONDSON
Covenant Connections Church
Flowery Branch, Georgia

7

The Three Duties of Every Believer

When you do a charitable deed...your Father who
sees in secret will Himself reward you openly.
When you pray...your Father who sees
in secret will reward you openly.
When you fast...your Father who sees
in secret will reward you openly.
—MATTHEW 6:3-4,6,17-18

THE THREE DUTIES OF EVERY BELIEVER ARE TO GIVE, TO PRAY, and to fast. These words are the teachings of Jesus that He taught hundreds of times and are recorded in the Sermon on the Mount. Jesus did not say "if" but "when" you give, pray, and fast. These spiritual disciplines are obligations as Christians.

Then Jesus couples to each of these duties a blessing. "The Father who sees in secret will reward you openly." If you read a particular verse written in red—the words Jesus spoke—you know it is important. If the same verse is mentioned twice, it's a Hebrew way of saying, "If you don't get anything else, get this: 'The Father who sees in secret will reward you openly.'"

However, in this case it's mentioned three times. God wants you to know He gives king-sized bonuses when you pray, give, and fast.

There's a blessing and reward when you give. There's a different reward when you pray than when you give. There is also a separate reward when someone fasts.

If a person only prays, they will get a reward. Jeremiah 33:3 says, "Call unto me, and I will answer thee, and show thee great and mighty things, which thou knowest not" (KJV). Prayer has great rewards, but it is only a 30-fold blessing. Because it is not mixed with fasting and giving, prayers are often slow in being answered or are too weak to pierce the darkness of evil, and they go unanswered.

However, when someone adds giving and tithing to their prayers, it produces not only the reward of prayer, but also the reward of giving. This equals a 60-fold blessing. Giving releases the abundance of Heaven that does not happen through prayer alone. Jesus said, "Give, and it shall be given unto you; good measure, pressed down, and shaken together, and running over" (Luke 6:38 KJV).

Malachi 3:10 demands us to:

> *Bring ye all the tithes into the storehouse, that there may be meat in mine house, and prove me now herewith, saith the Lord of hosts, if I will not open you the windows of heaven, and pour you out a blessing, that there shall not be room enough to receive it* (KJV).

Notice the Scripture says "the Lord of hosts." The literal meaning in Hebrew is "Lord of armies"—*tza-va* (צבא) is the word for army—and what today refers to the Israeli Defense Force. In this case, it means "the Army of Angels." Some versions translate the phrase as "Lord of the Angel Armies." In other words, when you tithe and give offerings, it attracts angels to fight for you.

Jacob made a vow to God that he would always be a tither. His Uncle Laban cheated him ten times. However, Jacob continued to honor God in his giving. One night, an angel of prosperity appeared to him in a dream and gave him a business plan that made him a multi-millionaire (see Gen. 31:11). The angel of prosperity stayed with Jacob all his life and then continued to bless his children after Jacob's death. This angel is one of the blessings of giving and does not come with prayer alone.

The third duty is fasting. Fasting means not to eat. One does not fast television or fast going to the movies. That's not fasting. That's abstinence. Fasting is not eating food. Jesus said in Mark 2:20 when the bridegroom is taken away, "Then shall they fast in those days" (KJV). Jesus was crucified on a Friday. Because of this, the church traditionally had Friday as the day of fasting.

Curses, weaknesses, and strongholds are broken when a person fasts. Strangleholds and viselike grips satan has on families—such as divorce, poverty, cancer, drugs, and addictions, etc.—become broken-off homes when people add fasting to their spiritual disciplines.

Fasting becomes a continual prayer. When one fasts one 24-hour day, it is equivalent to 24 hours of prayer. If you prayed one hour each day for one year, that is 365 hours of prayer. Each year we do a 21-day fast. This is 501 hours of fasting, which is a continual prayer. This long fast becomes equal to over a year of prayer.

When one gives, prays, and fasts, it releases the hundred-fold blessing, where nothing is impossible to you.

Dr. Bob Rodgers
Author and lead pastor, Evangel World Prayer Center
Louisville, Kentucky

8

When Heaven Invades Earth

Our Debt to the World: An Encounter with God

Jesus was walking down a crowded road with people from all sides trying to get close to Him. A woman reached out and touched His garment. He stopped and asked, "Who touched Me?" The disciples were startled by such a question because to them, it had been such an obvious answer—everyone! But Jesus went on to say that He felt virtue (*dunamis*) flow from Him. He was anointed by the Holy Spirit. The actual power of the Spirit of God left His being and flowed into that woman and healed her. The anointing was resident in Jesus' physical body the same as with every believer. The faith of that woman put a demand on that anointing in Jesus. She was healed because *the anointing breaks the yoke.*

A very popular verse for receiving an offering is, "Freely you have received, freely give." But the context of the verse is often forgotten. Jesus was referring to the ministry of the supernatural. Listen to the implication: "I have received something that I am to give away!" What? The Holy Spirit. He is the greatest gift anyone could ever receive. And He is living in me.

When we minister in the anointing, we actually give away the presence of God—we impart Him to others. Jesus went on to teach His disciples what it meant to *give it away*. It included the obvious things, such as healing the sick, casting out demons, etc. But it also included one of the forgotten aspects: "When you go into a house…let your peace come up on it" (Matt. 10:12-13). There is an actual impartation of His presence that we are able to make in these situations. This is how we bring the lost into an encounter with God. We learn to recognize His presence, cooperate with His passion for people, and invite them to receive *salvation*.

He has made us stewards of the presence of God. It is not as though we can manipulate and use His presence for our own religious purposes. We are moved upon by the Holy Spirit, thereby becoming co-laborers with Christ. In that position we invite Him to invade the circumstances that arise before us.

The more obvious ways are in preaching or praying for people's specific needs. Don't underestimate this important tool. By looking for chances to serve, we give the Holy Spirit the opportunity to do what only He can do—miracles. I don't see everyone I pray for healed. I'm not batting even close to a thousand. But there are many more healed than would be had I not prayed for anyone!

Give God a chance to do what only He can do. He looks for those who are willing to be *smeared* with Him, allowing His presence to affect others for good. A visiting minister recently told us, "The difference between you and me is this: if I pray for a dead person and they are not raised from the dead, I pray for the next dead person too. I don't quit!"

Jesus said, "If I do not do the works of My Father, do not believe Me." The works of the Father are miracles. Even the Son of God stated it was the miraculous that validated His ministry on earth. In that context, He said, "he who believes in Me...greater works than these he will do, because I go to my Father" (John 14:12). The miraculous is a large part of the plan of God for this world. And it is to come through the Church.

I look forward to the day when the Church stands up and says, "Don't believe us unless we're doing the works that Jesus did!" The Bible says that we are to pursue earnestly (lustfully!) spiritual gifts, and that those gifts make us *established*. Which ones? All of them.

BILL JOHNSON
Author and lead pastor, Bethel Church
Redding, California

9

Carrying the Presence of Revival

REVIVAL IS AN AWAKENING TO THE PRESENCE AND THE GLORY of God in a believer's life. The Lord comes upon us and we become fully aware of Him. Many times, we experience His manifested presence much like the priests in the days of Solomon as He "weighed" upon them. Just as the ministers of Israel literally *could not stand* because of His presence resting on them (see 2 Chron. 7:1-3), we too find it difficult to stand under the weight of His glory! However, for us, the "standing" is not literal, but spiritual.

Dr. Todd Smith, pastor and author of *Speaking in Tongues: Your Secret Weapon*, said, "Before God sits down on a place, He measures its capacity. He takes the temperature." We all know what temperature measures, but what about capacity? Capacity is the maximum amount something can hold or something's *ability to hold*. As the temple of the presence of God, the Lord has to check our capacity, our ability to hold His glory, before He will sit down on us in the fullness of His power.

Can we carry Him? Can we stand up under the weight of His glory? Can we house His power? Do we have the *capacity* to host His presence? In order to answer these questions, He has to measure our *ability to hold!* To do this, He must examine our heart. In Romans 8:27, the Bible says, "Now He who searches the hearts knows what the mind of the Spirit is." What is it that He is looking for? He is looking for weak areas, those areas in our lives where we are fractured, broken, or compromised.

The Lord knows if we are broken or fractured in our heart, we will not be able to carry His weighty glory! He has to shed light on those areas so we may be healed and able to carry His presence. That is our purpose—to carry His revival glory to the world—but if we are broken or fractured in heart, the weight of His glory will crush us. It is in His mercy that He holds back all the fullness of revival presence until we are healthy and stable enough to host Him.

Think about it this way. Physically speaking, a fracture is a crack in a bone. There are four categories of fractures—simple, compound, non-displaced, and displaced. With a simple fracture, the bone is broken, but the flesh is not punctured. In the spirit, we can have a simple fracture, that small area showing a hairline break, tiny and almost unnoticed, and it hasn't punctured the flesh! In other words, we can hide it pretty well, but it is a fracture nonetheless. And left unattended, it will only get worse.

A compound fracture is when the bone is broken and it has punctured the flesh. In other words, everyone can see the broken bone! Spiritually speaking, has that ever been the case in your life? There is a spiritual fracture in your heart and it is so severe that it is showing in your flesh? Ouch!

The next two types of fractures are the displaced and non-displaced fractures. A non-displaced fracture is when the bone is broken, *but it is still aligned.* Again, spiritually speaking, we can have a non-displaced fracture in our heart. There is a broken place, but we are fully aware of the need for healing and repentance and we move quickly to allow the Lord to mend that area. Last, there is the displaced fracture. In the spirit, this is the worst break. The bone is totally broken and out of alignment. This happens in a heart that has carried a hurt or offense for so long that they can no longer hear the word of the Lord in the matter. Surgery is needed.

I believe you are beginning to understand this illustration. In the natural, bones give us structure. It is no different in the spirit. If we have a strong spiritual structure, we will have the capacity to carry all God intends for us to carry. If we have broken places of offense, hurt, unforgiveness, or bitterness, our structure will be compromised and we will fold.

God, in His mercy, will not put more of His glory us than we can hold. We all want to hold all that He has for us, but in order to carry it, we must allow Him to mend the broken places in our heart. This will only make us strong in the spirit and able to *house* all that He has for us.

Decide today to lay prostrate before the Lord under His supernatural x-ray machine and allow Him to check your life and heart for any weak areas, broken places, or infection. Then and only then can we begin the surgical process of healing so we may carry His presence and revival to the world!

KAREN SMITH
President, KINEO Ministry Training Center
Christ Fellowship Church
Dawsonville, Georgia
www.kineomtc.com

10

Never Get Over Jesus!

I WAS RAISED IN CHURCHES AND A CHRISTIAN FAMILY WHO were wild for God and everything that meant. We prayed for hours. We never missed a church service. We went to extra meetings. And every day, my sister and I were required to read four chapters of the Bible—and were quizzed on them! Then, when I was eight years old, Jesus pulled me up to Heaven for a visit; and when I was twelve, He visited me and told me to write about *God's Generals*. Maybe it was my upbringing, or maybe it was those times I was around Him in the flesh, but I have never gotten over Jesus.

Jesus is more than my Lord and Savior or some religious figurehead; He is my best friend. This close relationship really began during my visit to Heaven. Here's what happened when I first saw Him:

> I know it's not nice to stare, but I can't stop staring at Him. My legs crumble, and I fall on my knees in front of him. Everything in me cries for joy. Tears stream down my face. I cannot stop them.
>
> He says, "Now stop the tears. It's time to go through Heaven. I want to give you a tour through Heaven, because I love you so much."

I hear and feel His words at the same time, and His words change me on the inside, like joy exploding. I can't stop crying. He's too wonderful! He says, "No need of tears, but a face full of joy would make Me glad." He laughs—a deep belly laugh—and I do too! He reaches down, takes hold of me, and draws me up to stand in front of Him. He wipes away my tears with His fingers.

He loves me, and He likes me. I'm not scared at all! I realize who He is, but it isn't like being with a famous person on earth. I'm totally calm.

I've never gotten over Jesus, and I have read about and known men and women of God who never had a personal encounter with Him and also never got over Him. Frankly, I don't think those who do get over Him ever really came to know Him as the Living Word. They never went into the printed page to see Him and hear Him. Reading and studying the Bible was a religious ritual instead of a spiritual encounter with their very best friend. What was it Jesus said?

> *It is the Spirit who gives life; the flesh profits nothing; the words that I have spoken to you are spirit and are life* (John 6:63 NASB).

To know Jesus in a living, breathing way, we have to live by the Spirit. Our natural minds cannot understand how Jesus is the Word. We can only understand by the Holy Spirit in our spirits. It is the Holy Spirit who opens our hearts and minds to see Jesus as He really is. He's the way, the truth, and the life (see John 14:6). He Himself is our path to the Father. Truth for us is not an idea or a concept; truth is a Person. And He is our eternal life. In Him we live and move and exist (see Acts 17:28).

Beloved, do you live and move and exist in Jesus, or are you over Him? Did you forget how He saved you and brought you out of the kingdom of darkness? Have you been so blessed that you have gotten over how desperate you were to be rescued from your selfishness, foolishness, and sin?

The Church is revived as each one of us remembers who Jesus is to us. He's not someone you nod to on Sundays and forget about during the week. He's everything to you in every moment of your day. All you have to do is look in the Living Word to:

- see Him on the Cross and remember His and your Father's love for you,
- see Him taking the keys of death and Hell from the devil, stripping him of all authority over you,
- see Him being resurrected and know your sin is washed away and you are free!

Jesus did all this for *you*. He saved you, and then He placed you in His Body. He gave you spiritual mothers, fathers, sisters, and brothers. Not only is He with you forever, but so are the ones He placed in your life. He gave them to you and you to them to share and grow in the gifts and callings He gave you. He gave you a purpose! He made you a vital part of His plan to cover the earth with His glory.

Beloved, never get over Jesus!

ROBERTS LIARDON
Author, church historian, revivalist
Pastor, Embassy International Church, Orlando, Florida

11

The Unveiling of the Church

*I am convinced that any suffering we endure is less
than nothing compared to the magnitude of glory
that is about to be unveiled within us. The entire
universe is standing on tiptoe, yearning to see the
unveiling of God's glorious sons and daughters!*
—ROMANS 8:18-19 TPT

WHEN I HEAR THE WORD *UNVEILING*, ONE OF THE FIRST
things that I imagine is the unveiling of the bride at a wedding. Traditionally the bride is walked down the aisle by her father, and then with eager anticipation all onlookers await as the father lifts the veil. This is a powerful moment in the wedding, and the most meaningful moment for the father of the bride. The father's heart is filled with gladness and joy as the groom and all other onlookers behold the radiant beauty of his daughter—the bride unveiled.

Scripture says that in a similar way, the heart's desire of our heavenly Father is to unveil the radiant beauty of His sons and daughters to the world. And according to God's Word, the byproduct of this unveiling will be revival. When people see clearly the goodness and glory of God through His glorious sons and daughters, they will come flocking to receive the salvation, deliverance, and healing of the Lord. Let me say that again—*revival is the product of God's glory being unveiled to the world through His loving, beautiful, radiant, powerful sons and daughters.*

So the next logical question must be, "What must we do to be unveiled by God?" Simple. Get ready. God only unveils those who are willing and ready. Unveiling (or revealing) sons and daughters who are not yet ready to be unveiled would be embarrassing to us and would have a negative effect on an onlooking world. In the same way that a bride prepares to be unveiled for a wedding, we are to prepare to be unveiled by God. So how can we do that?

Our answer is found in Matthew 25:1-13. In this passage of Scripture Jesus tells a story about ten bridesmaids and how five of them were ready and five were not. In this passage He defines readiness as those who have "extra oil." It was only the bridesmaids with extra oil in their lamps who were allowed to go enjoy a feast with Jesus. When the others finally acquired some oil, it was too late.

Obviously, this parable can be used in many different contexts, but it is clear that one interpretation of this text is that Jesus is describing a special ministry opportunity that is only available for those with "extra oil." The virgins are obviously symbolic of the whole Church. They are all pure, but only half of them were prepared at His coming. The oil is very important in this Scripture. The oil in this passage is symbolic of the Holy Spirit in the context of intimacy. The bridegroom,

Jesus, told the unprepared bridesmaids that He did not know them. That word for *know* in the Greek means "to know intimately" or "to kiss." The point that Jesus is making is that the most important resource you can acquire for ministry is time spent with Him.

I truly believe that the next great revival will be the product of God unveiling those who have spent much time acquiring oil from Him. Those who are on fire for His presence. Those who worship Him more in private than in public. Those who wear out the carpet pacing and praying. Those who are logging hundreds of hours in prayer closets and prayer meetings. Those who consume His words like it is their last meal. Those who drink from His love in the secret place like it is their last drink.

I believe that God is inviting His people (right now) to begin filling their lamps with extra oil and to prepare themselves for what is coming—the dramatic unveiling, or appearing, of God's sons and daughters with the glory of Jesus upon them. And everyone who sees our love for Him will desire to experience the same. Let's get ready for the great unveiling!

MATT SCOTT
Lead pastor, The Gathering Place Church
Moody, Alabama
www.gpchurch.tv

12

Revival's Impact upon Theology

I TEACH A COURSE AT THE GLOBAL AWAKENING THEOLOGICAL Seminary—*Christian Theologies.* This course focuses on how revivals impact theology. It is a course that is based in historical theology, from the book of Acts till today, with a special focus on revival's impact upon theology. I want to share about the theological emphasis of the revival that was one of the four most important revivals of the 1990s; the influence of this revival continues to this day through the people who were touched in it. They continue to carry revival around the world and their spiritual sons and daughters are set to be the primary carriers of revival in the next generation and its revival.

This revival would be called many things—the Laughing Revival, the Toronto Blessing, the Father's Blessing, the Pensacola Outpouring or the Brownsville Revival, the revival among evangelical colleges, and the Smithton Outpouring. Many view these as separate revivals, but I see them as manifestations of one great outpouring beginning with Claudio Freidzon in Buenos Aires, Argentina, 1992; Rodney Howard-Browne in Lakeland, Florida, 1993; then John Arnott and me in Toronto, Canada, January 20, 1994;

Eleanor Mumford, England, May 1995; Steve Hill and John Kilpatrick in Brownsville, Florida, May 1995; Steve Gray in Smithton, Missouri, 1996; Rolland and Heidi Baker, Pemba, Mozambique, 1997; Bill Johnson, Bethel, California, 1997; and beginning in 1999 the influence on many networks and denominations in Brazil.

Once again, this revival produced millions of souls being saved, scores of thousands of new churches being started, and a focus on the Father's heart, healing, prophecy, and equipping the saints. The missionary work of Rolland and Heidi Baker would be greatly impacted by what happened to them in Toronto and the prophetic word given to Heidi. Leif Hetland's missionary work, through mass crusades, in Pakistan would likewise be powerfully impacted through the laying on of hands and a prophetic word for him. Missions would become a major theme of the revival with a quarter of the sermons I preached during the first several years being on missions and the relationship between missions and revival.

I was sharing about the impact of this revival once in England when one of the key leaders in Alpha said, "Why don't you talk about Alpha as one of the influences of the Toronto Blessing?" I told him that I wasn't aware there was a connection. He told me that Alpha really took off right after the Toronto Blessing, and there was a connection. I knew that Rev. Nicki Gumble had been profoundly touched by the Vineyard movement through John Wimber, but I didn't know Alpha had been impacted through the Toronto Blessing.

Then there would be the fruit of the culture changing of Bethel Church in Redding, California. Pastor Bill Johnson would be powerfully impacted and influenced by the Spirit of God and the friendship and relationship he would have with key leaders of the Toronto Blessing. Through Bill the emphasis on the goodness of God would become a theological impact. Worship is always impacted by revival, and there was a powerful influence on worship that arose out of Bethel church.

The following became strong theological emphases of this revival: *Missions,* especially through Rolland and Heidi Baker, Leif Hetland, Ché Ahn, and me; *the Father's heart* through John and Carol Arnott; *the goodness of God* through Bill Johnson; *the importance of healing and signs and wonders to the proper proclamation of the Gospel* through Bill Johnson and me; *the joy of the Lord* through Georgian and Winnie Banov; and the primary message and theological emphasis of my own ministry has been that of *impartation through the laying on of hands, sometimes accompanied by prophecy.* All of the members of the Revival Alliance—Rolland and Heidi Baker, Ché and Sue Ahn, John and Carol Arnott, Georgian and Winnie Banov, Bill and Beni Johnson, and DeAnne and I—were impacted through the power of impartation in this revival. But not only were we touched, Evangelist Steve Hill was touched in London at the Holy Trinity Brompton Anglican Church on his was to Lakeland, Florida, while Lindell Cooley and John Kilpatrick's wife were touched powerfully in Toronto.

This revival ended in Toronto after twelve and a half years of nightly meetings six nights a week, but the revival itself has continued through the work of those who were powerfully impacted and went to the nations and are influencing our nation. The work I have been involved with since 1999 in

Brazil is ever increasing with the number of very large multiple thousand-member churches increasing dramatically in the last two years, especially among the traditional Baptists.

The overriding theological emphases of this revival have been the importance of healings, miracles, deliverances, salvations, social ministry, church planting, equipping the saints, and renewal of other denominations and movements. There has been the desire to reunite the personal and social aspects of the Gospel that were separated in the 1920s with the modernist-fundamentalist controversy.

Let us be faithful to carry the fire that God has entrusted to the leaders of this revival. May we finish the course and have much fruit and trophies of grace through transformed lives to lay at the Master's feet. Pray and work in faith for revival!

RANDY CLARK, D.D., D.MIN., TH.D., M.DIV.
President and adjunct professor, Global
Awakening Theological Seminary
Overseer of the Apostolic Network of Global Awakening
Author of over 40 books, including *Destined for
the Cross, Eyewitness to Miracles, Stories of Divine
Healing, Authority to Heal, Power to Heal, The Healing
Breakthrough, Baptized in the Spirit, There Is More, The
Essential Guide to the Power of the Holy Spirit,* and more

13

You Are Revival!

"Now, Lord, consider their threats and enable your
servants to speak your word with great boldness.
Stretch out your hand to heal and perform signs
and wonders through the name of your holy servant
Jesus." After they prayed, the place where they were
meeting was shaken. And they were all filled with
the Holy Spirit and spoke the word of God boldly.
—ACTS 4:29-31 NIV

WILLIAM BOOTH, THE FOUNDER OF THE SALVATION ARMY, said, "I'm not waiting for a move of God; I am a move of God." It's time for Spirit-empowered believers to stop looking for revival and realize you are the revival God wants to pour out on this world.

John Wesley, the founder of the Methodist church, after his Aldersgate experience when his heart was strangely warmed, went out and began preaching the fire of God. He did not seek more experiences; instead, he became revival, and the First Great Awakening was underway. Wesley was so successful that within 150 years, there were more Methodists than the population of England in his day.

Charles Finney, the towering figure of the Second Great Awakening, was a lawyer who experienced liquid waves of God's love washing over him. After this experience, he did not feel the need to seek more experiences but took what he had and gave it away. He spoke the word with simplicity using everyday illustrations to help others receive what he had been given. By the end of his life, he had led a million souls into the Kingdom. Both Wesley and Finney did not seek revival; they became revival.

Charles Spurgeon said, "A hale and hearty young man has no need of revival. No one thinks of reviving the noonday sun. A tree planted by the rivers of water loaded with fruit needs not excite our anxiety for its revival, for its fruitfulness charms everyone. So it is with the children of God who lay down in green pastures, they have no need to cry, 'woe is me, the leanness of my soul!'" Beloved, as an on-fire believer, you need not pray for more fire; instead, share the fire you already have!

You have God's power! Revival is the resurrection of the dead. The same power that raised Jesus from the dead lives in you! You need not look to outside sources for revival. Fix your eyes on Jesus, the true source who has graciously and lovingly given you His Holy Spirit. He has already given you all power and authority. He has already seated you in heavenly places where you rule and reign in life with Him. Realize who you are in Christ and who Christ is in you, and be the revival this world is looking for.

The Kingdom of God is upside down from the kingdom of this world. In God's Kingdom, the more you give away, the more you have to give. If you want more of God, give away what you have, and more will be given. Jesus told his disciples, "Go, proclaim this message: 'The kingdom of heaven has come near.' Heal the sick, raise the dead, cleanse those who have leprosy, drive out demons. Freely you have received; freely give" (Matt. 10:7-8 NIV).

The vibrant church of Acts, after being filled with the Holy Spirit, did not pray for another experience. Instead, they prayed for greater boldness to perform healings, signs, and wonders, then went out and spoke the word of God boldly.

The Spirit of the Lord is upon you. He has anointed you to be the revival this lost world needs. Don't let the enemy rob you another day of the anointing you already have. Believe and receive, then release what you already have. You are revival!

CONNIE DAWSON, PH.D.
Lead pastor, Radiant Church
Lincoln, Nebraska

14

God Loves the Smell of Death!

For thus says the High and Lofty One who inhabits eternity, whose name is Holy: "I dwell in the high and holy place, with him who has a contrite and humble spirit, to revive the spirit of the humble, and to revive the heart of the contrite ones."

—Isaiah 57:15

RECENTLY, I CRIED OUT TO GOD FOR AN INCREASE OF HIS glory in my life; He immediately responded, "Increase your brokenness." I wasn't expecting that quick of a response and certainly not that straightforward of an answer. He quickly let me know He would love to give me more but it came at a price. I have discovered there is no shortcut to revival, and the glory of God comes at a high price. As the host pastor of the North Georgia Revival I have learned nothing attracts God more than an individual being broken over his/her sinfulness.

Tommy Tenney in his book *The God Chasers* said, "The more death that God smells, the closer He can come."[1] There is something about dying or burning flesh that God likes. I don't know about you, but to me burning flesh is atrocious.

Very few stenches in the world are more repulsive; however, the Bible says when the animal sacrifices were being burned on the altar the Lord smelled a sweet, soothing aroma (see Gen. 8:21; Exod. 29:18; Lev. 1:17; Eph. 5:2). The burning of flesh is not repulsive to God, but He draws near it.

Spiritually speaking, our flesh prevents God's glory from manifesting and limits the release of His full work of power in our life. However, when we crawl up on the altar and cry out for Him to consume us with His holy fire, He burns the sinful debris. The more flesh He consumes, the more glory we walk in.

This is painful and people, if possible, avoid it.

Kathryn Kuhlman (1907–1976) was a powerful woman of God who traveled the world sharing Christ and demonstrated an amazing healing ministry. She preached an uncompromising Gospel and demonstrated the power of the Kingdom as many blind, crippled, deaf, and diseased were dramatically healed. She carefully revealed in a sermon the price she had to pay to have such a powerful healing ministry:

> It costs everything. If you really want to know the price, it will cost you everything. Kathryn Kuhlman died a long time ago. I know the day; I know the hour. I can go to the spot where Kathryn Kuhlman died. For me it was easy because I had nothing. I know better than anyone else from whence I come, a little cross-road town in Missouri, a population of 1,200 people. I had nothing. I was born without talent. Most people are born with something. I didn't even have hair on my head when I was born, just red fuzz. One

day I just looked up and said, "Wonderful Jesus, I have nothing. I have nothing to give You but my love. That's all I can give You. And I love You with all my heart. I give You my body, a living sacrifice. If You can take nothing and use it, then here is nothing. Take it." It isn't silver vessels He is asking for; it isn't golden vessels that He needs. He just needs yielded vessels.[2]

She also said it takes tremendous sacrifice. "Its terms require a surrender which the average Christian is unwilling to make. Things that are gotten cheap are usually cheap. The things you have to pay most for are usually the things that are most valuable."[3]

It is this level of abandonment that attracts the glory of God to humanity. Nothing short of full unequivocal surrender and denial. A.B. Simpson summed it up best: "We must surrender ourselves so utterly that we can never own ourselves again. We must hand over self and all its rights in an eternal covenant and give God the absolute right to own us, control us and possess us forever."

Here is a thought you don't hear very often. You and I get to determine the amount of glory we want in our lives. I want as much as my flesh can handle—the more broken and shattered I am in His presence the more I can carry!

TODD SMITH
Christ Fellowship Church
Dawsonville, Georgia
North Georgia Revival
www.kingdomready.tv

Notes

1. Tommy Tenney, *The God Chasers* (Shippensburg, PA: Destiny Image Publishers, 1998), 60.

2. "Kathryn Kuhlman It will cost you everything," Women of Purpose and Destiny, YouTube, July 20, 2018, https://www.youtube.com/watch?v=wkuvXqVz-xc.

3. Ibid.

15

Sustaining a Move of the Holy Spirit

THERE ARE SO MANY ELEMENTS OF REVIVAL—PREPARING THE hearts of the leaders, preparing the hearts of the people, and prayer to our sovereign Lord asking that He would send a time of refreshing (see Acts 3:19; 2 Chron. 7:14). Carol and I were so privileged to have exactly that actually happen to us on January 20, 1994. The Holy Spirit descended upon us with a violent, glorious, powerful joy that continues to this day. That is what I want to share with you in this devotional time, as we continue and grow together in the glorious presence of the Holy Spirit.

Years ago, I read a book by Dr. Yonggi Cho called *The Fourth Dimension*. He was majoring on prayer, but made a startling statement that really stuck with me: "Revivals are never supposed to end." But sadly, they usually do for a number of reasons. The leaders tire out, or fall out with one another, or fall into sin or heresy.[1] But the heart of God is that revival should continue, grow, and expand, as it did in the book of Acts. When revival fell on us suddenly, there were many voices coaching us, all with the best of intentions, saying be sure to do this and be sure not to do that. Many were not helpful, but a couple of them were. I remember John Wimber saying this: "You don't get to keep it until you give it away." That phrase echoed the words of Jesus for me when He said, "Freely you have received, freely give" (Matt. 10:8). We developed a very high value on freely giving and imparting the anointing to all who came. We had over 4.5 million people come during 12½ years of nightly meetings. Sharing and imparting the anointing was and is a very high value.

Another very helpful word of advice came from Margaret Poloma, a sociologist from the University of Akron Ohio. She is practiced in the psychology and sociology of revival and of the workings of the Holy Spirit throughout historical revivals, although I did not know that when I first met her. She asked to survey the people who were being powerfully touched by God. I hesitated, as I did not want a sociologist telling me from a secular point of view that it was all psychosomatic and the power of suggestion. But in the end we proceeded, and her results were music to my ears. She surveyed 989 people from both sexes, various age groups, and different national backgrounds and levels of education. They had all been touched by the awesome power of the Holy Spirit and freely volunteered to take part in her survey. Her results were wonderfully surprising and so confirming.

Of the people surveyed, 93 percent said, "As a result of being deeply touched by the Holy Spirit, I am now more in love with Jesus than I have ever been in my life." The second highest response was given by 87 percent of the people who said, "As a result of being powerfully touched by the Holy Spirit, I am more excited about sharing Jesus with my family and friends than I have ever been in all my life." This was such a wonderful confirmation to me. It was reflecting the great commandment from Matthew 22:37—love the Lord your God with all your heart, with all your soul, and with all your mind, and second, love your neighbor as yourself.

Margaret left me with some extremely helpful words of wisdom. She shared with me that in every revival, there is a very real tension between the free-flowing charisma of the Holy Spirit and the forces of institutionalization as people, leaders, and critics all try to "tidy it up." She said, "This is what always kills a revival, and it will eventually end yours too, but my advice is resist that strongly as long as you can." In other words, continue to let God have His way, and use who He chooses, and let it go where He wants it to go. Don't mess with it too much, but keep it on track and within Scripture.

JOHN ARNOTT
Catch the Fire Toronto

Note

1. There is a very helpful book by Arthur Wallis entitled *In the Day of Thy Power,* which points out why the New Hebrides revival and the Welsh revival were relatively short-lived.

16

Prophetic Promises of Greater Glory

WE ARE NOW 26 YEARS DOWN THE ROAD IN REVIVAL. THE Holy Spirit is still coming in power and love, filling people, healing people, and transforming lives, marriages, and families. It has now spread all over the earth, and do you know what else? There is another powerful wave about to come very soon. David Ruis prophesied in our Catch the Fire conference back in October 1994, saying, "If you think this is it, it is not it. You have seen nothing yet. I am merely growing up a plant that will go to seed and My winds will blow that seed to the ends of the earth. That seed will germinate and grow and become the mightiest harvest and move of God the world has ever seen."[1]

There is a mighty move of God about to visit planet Earth, friends. Many prophecies have predicted that it will begin in 2020. As I write this, most of the world is quarantined and restricted to their homes. Something massive is brewing. When revival hits, it will be a *suddenly*, perhaps ten times more powerful than anything we have ever seen. Promise yourself not to react in fear or try to tidy it up and tailor it to your comfort zone. Allow the young people, the women, and indeed everybody to step fully into that river and go with it wherever the river flows. That's where the life is (see Ezek. 47:9). A billion souls are about to come into the Kingdom (see Rev. 14:14)!

Oh, and one more thing. Smith Wigglesworth prophesied back in 1947 that the final revival would be the Word and the Spirit together. Getting into heresy, false doctrine, sin, and immorality will kill revival perhaps quicker than anything else. Now is the time for all of us, especially our youth, to get into the Word of God and to know the whole counsel of God as it is revealed in all of Scripture. Don't get your theology from sound bites and other secondhand teaching methods only. Get into the Word of God yourself, read it, meditate on it, memorize it, know it, and get it deeply into your spirit. It is vitally important that revival stays within the clear teaching and revelation of the Bible. Allow the Holy Spirit to be your primary teacher, and stay humble before the Lord with clean hands and a pure heart (see Ps. 24:4).

Get ready young people—you're going to be leading it!

JOHN ARNOTT
Catch the Fire Toronto

Note

1. "David Ruis Prophecy October 1994," Scott Jones, YouTube, January 26, 2014, https://www.youtube.com/watch?v =6FDTlNGVgeo.

17

Reckless Abandonment

I HAVE DISCOVERED A COMMON THREAD AMONG MANY OF the heroes of faith and especially Moses and David. From the Old Testament to the New Testament, the men and women who changed nations and advanced God's Kingdom refused to settle for a status-quo relationship with God. They were just common, everyday people like you and me, but they had a very uncommon pursuit of God. They wanted more than blessings and more than a general understanding of God. When they encountered God, they abandoned all and pursued God with a relentless passion that would not be denied. Their priorities were to know God intimately, live in His presence, and fulfill His will no matter their circumstances or the cost.

When God's presence manifested on the mountain with lighting, thunder, and darkness in Exodus 20:18-21, the people drew back and told Moses to go and speak with God, but they did not want God to speak directly to them. Moses went immediately in to the thick darkness where God's presence was. Moses would not allow the stormy environment or the reaction of the people to affect his pursuit of God's presence.

In Exodus 33:1-18, God promised to give Israel the promised land but declared His presence would not go with them.

To Moses this was not acceptable, because Moses wanted more than the blessings of God—he wanted God. Moses understood that he had found favor in the sight of the Lord, but that was not enough! He declared he must know why he had found favor and asked God to show him His ways and His glory, declaring he would not take one step without His presence. We must have a determination to know His ways and fully see His glory. We are created in the image of God, and we cannot reflect His image and nature if we have not fully seen, known, and experienced Him.

We see the same reckless abandonment from David as he pursued God with a diligence that would not be denied. David refused to let how his family viewed him keep him from doing the right thing and fighting Goliath and killing the giant that defied the armies of Israel. In Psalm 25, David appears to be greatly troubled and surrounded by his enemies, but in these difficulties he cries out to God, "Show me Your ways" (Ps. 25:4). David desired to know God in the deepest of ways. He never allowed personal failure, disappointment, personal loss, or even delayed promises to prevent him from obedience and persistent pursuit of God and His presence. When David became king and experienced the fulfilment of God's promises to him, it was not enough! He must have the presence of God and with reckless abandonment recovered and restored back to Israel the Ark of the Covenant, which represented the manifest presence of God.

We must have a generation of Christians who will not settle for status-quo Christianity but will with reckless abandonment pursue to know God intimately, to live in His presence, and to do His will no matter the cost. God has made this obtainable by the death and resurrection of His glorious Son, Jesus. His blood cleansed us so that that God Himself through the Holy Spirit could come and live in us (see John 14:23). He made His throne of grace approachable and His voice to be heard. He has empowered us to be the sons and daughters of God who advance and build His glorious Kingdom. You are created to conquer and overcome; He has chosen you to bear His glorious image so that the world can see Him in love, power, and authority. If this generation will humble themselves and go after Him with reckless abandonment and pursue Him with a tenacity and consistency that will not be denied, we will be the next great awakening and world-sweeping revival.

> *God, stir us till there is a hunger to know You like never before and a passion to live and abide in Your presence every day and our greatest desire is to fulfill Your perfect will. Give us the grace to lay down our lives so we can pursue You with reckless abandonment.*

LANCE JOHNSON
Relevate Church
Ranger, Georgia

18

The One New Man: A Hidden Key for Revival

IS THE ONE NEW MAN A HIDDEN KEY FOR REVIVAL? I THINK it is.

In Ephesians 2, the apostle Paul teaches us that through the death of Jesus, the ultimate act of covenant sacrifice, the Father created in Himself "one new man" or "one new humanity." Through His life, death, and subsequently the birth of the early Church (which was in fact a One New Man movement), we see the first revival fires beginning to burn.

Unique things happen when Jews and Gentiles work together. Let's look at history for a moment:

- Boaz and Ruth the Moabitess (the great grandparents of King David)
- Caleb and Joshua (some believe Caleb had Gentile roots)
- Peter and Cornelius and the band of Italian (Gentile) soldiers
- Paul, Barnabas, and Silas all went to the Gentile nations as biblical examples of Jews

and Gentiles operating spiritually as One New Man.

- The Great Commission where the 11 Jewish disciples were commissioned to make disciples of all nations, immersing them into the Father, Son, and Holy Spirit.

- Christopher Columbus (believed to have been Jewish because his diary was written in Hebrew) and his Spanish and Jewish crew traveled to the New World.

- George Washington borrowed money from Haym Salomon, a Jewish lender, to build an army to fight against the British for independence.

- Abraham Lincoln enlisted Abraham Jonas, a Jewish man, as a legal and political associate and advisor during the time surrounding the Civil War.

Many times when God brings Jews and Gentiles together, there is a profound historic shift. The same can be said of Gentiles who helped the Jews during the Holocaust like Oskar Schindler and Corrie Ten Boom. Without Gentile help the nation of modern Israel might never have been born—which is, of course, the most prophetic event of the last century.

When we labor together, there is not only a profound shift in the natural, but also in the spirit.

You might remember the Pensacola Brownsville Revival, whose leadership included Pastor John Kilpatrick, a man of

Cherokee roots, as well as Dick Reuben and Michael Brown, who are both Jewish. Steve Hill also came to the revival as an evangelist preaching repentance like John the Baptist. You can see the pattern—John Kilpatrick, First Nations; Dick Reuben and Michael Brown, first-born Jews; Steve Hill, first-fruit Gentile. Their covenant agreement created a three-stranded cord of alignment that ushered in one of the largest revivals in recent history. This pattern is unmistakable. When you see God assembling leaders from various Gentile ethnicities with the Jewish people, it would be wise to get ready for a sovereign move!

> *For He Himself is our peace, who has made both one, and has broken down the middle wall of separation, having abolished in His flesh the enmity, that is, the law of commandments contained in ordinances, so as to create in Himself one new man from the two, thus making peace, and that He might reconcile them both to God in one body through the cross, thereby putting to death the enmity. And He came and preached peace to you who were afar off and to those who were near. For through Him we both have access by one Spirit to the Father.*
>
> *Now, therefore, you are no longer strangers and foreigners, but fellow citizens with the saints and members of the household of God, having been built on the foundation of the apostles and prophets, Jesus Christ Himself being the chief cornerstone, in whom the whole building, being fitted together, grows into a holy temple in the Lord,* ***in whom you***

also are being built together for a dwelling place of God in the Spirit (Ephesians 2:14-22).

This is the key—our unity creates a dwelling place for His Spirit, which is in essence revival. Our unity creates *shalom*—the Hebrew word for peace, which means nothing missing and nothing broken. When nothing is missing or broken, we have signs, wonders, healings, miracles, revival, and salvation—all key components to creating the atmosphere that builds a spiritual altar and a dwelling place for God as One New Man, thus making shalom.

Revival is shalom—and shalom is revival.

RABBI CURT LANDRY
House of David
Fairland, Oklahoma
www.curtlandry.com

19

Revival Fire Burns

Surely He has borne our griefs and carried our sorrows; yet we esteemed Him stricken, smitten by God, and afflicted. But He was wounded for our transgressions, He was bruised for our iniquities; the chastisement for our peace was upon Him, and by His stripes we are healed.

—ISAIAH 53:4-5

I HAVE BECOME CONSUMED WITH A LONGING FOR MORE OF God's presence. To know Christ and to make Him known.

In order to understand one of the deepest, almost hidden revelations concerning the Messiah, we have to get our minds around an ancient disease—leprosy.

Hansen's disease (also known as leprosy) is an infection caused by slow-growing bacteria called *Mycobacterium leprae*. It can affect the nerves, skin, eyes, and lining of the nose.

Leprosy, if left untreated, causes nerve damage, which can result in crippling of hands and feet, paralysis, and blindness.

A sinful church will lose its sight and ability to carry the Gospel to the World.

Biblical references to leprosy are powerful symbols reminding us of sin's spread and its horrible consequences. Like leprosy, sin starts out small but can then spread, leading to other sins and causing great damage to our relationship with God and others.

But the greatest problem with leprosy is the loss of pain. Without pain and suffering, we might be like lepers, unable to recognize that something is terribly wrong and that we need the healing touch of God.

Revival restores the pain of conviction to our lives.

Let us not be too quick to remove pain in our lives (whether physical, emotional, social, or spiritual pain). It may be God's megaphone to get our attention that something is seriously wrong and that we should flee to the One who created us.

Too many times we will not pay the painful price to remove connections with sin and we end up spiritually crippled and blind.

In Isaiah 53:4, we find *stricken*—a word used for one who is struck with leprosy. The rabbis in the Talmud concluded the Messiah will be called "the Leper of the House of Rabbi"—not an actual leper, but He would carry the "spiritual leprosy" of the people, as a leper carries his affliction.

The Messiah would come to a people who have lost their sensitivity to the sin that is killing them. People who have built up tolerance to the poison of sin and have even developed a taste and craving for its vile and bitter taste.

Scripture says that He, Jesus, would remove the blockers from our pain so that we can begin to heal. *No longer walking around numb to our pain but healed from our pain.*

When Jesus encountered lepers, what He gave them was the ability to feel again. *A church with a form of godliness will leave people in pain and shame, hard-hearted to sin.* Jesus wants to heal you. Let's look at how that will be accomplished: "But He was wounded for our transgressions."

Isaiah 53:5 could be translated, "In the fellowship of being one with Him is our healing." The pursuit of His presence, the call of revival builds our connection to Christ in whom our healing begins. We begin to feel the pain of our sin, the heartache of walking outside of receiving and granting forgiveness.

Revival fire burns when the fire of repentance burns within us.

Don C. Allen, PhD
The Church @ War Hill
Dawsonville, Georgia

20

The Roar Heard around the World

WILL YOU BE A LION FOR GOD, OR WILL YOU RUN FROM HIS assignment on your life? "The wicked flee though no one pursues, but the righteous are as bold as a lion" (Prov. 28:1). God is looking for those who will roar once again!

Today's church is at a massive crossroads. Will we choose revival, or will we choose cultural relevancy? Will we be carriers of the message of hope and freedom to a broken world desperately in need of an encounter with a savior named Jesus, or will we choose to be places of just powerless social gatherings where we are entertained by well-intentioned, gifted leaders who desire to grow a following but rarely make disciples? In order to be a disciple, one must die to the world and embrace their cross. You see, a sermon or talk will challenge you, but God's Spirit will awaken you (see Zech. 4:6).

The world is being destroyed by a liar and thief named satan. He has long seduced godly leaders into believing that the only way they will make their mark is by bowing to culture and embracing man's agenda. We are called to arise and lead. History is never made by those who choose to sit out the fight but by those who were willing to relinquish their fear and stand their ground against evil. We must awaken! The slumber of the bride has caused a release of the unprecedented plunder of God's storehouse and harvest by the enemy. He is now unabated by a church that once stood its ground but has now gone underground for fear of being exposed by our lack of purpose. For far too long the Spirit of God has often been locked outside our churches and left as a beggar in the street. For far too long we have minimalized the power of the Holy Spirit while all along embracing a form of secular Christianity.

The secret place has been dormant for far too long. I truly believe that God is whispering to His leaders (see Matt. 10:27) to come away and experience a refreshing for the journey and empowerment for the battle. You see, it is when you are away from the pulpit, the plaudits, and the programs that God can once again pour oil upon your head and place a fire in your belly. I have often said, "The greater the anointing, the greater the isolation." It is when God has hidden us for a season that He is able to shift our heart and spirit. In the day and age of platform-driven celebrity Christianity, we must once again go away into our secret place and allow God to transform us inside so we can touch the outside world for Him. After all, the very last chapter of the Bible sums up what God desires for each of us:

> *The Spirit and the bride say, "Come." Let him who hears say, "Come." Let him who is thirsty come. Let him who desires take the water of life freely* (Revelation 22:17 MEV).

Let me ask you today: Is there a cry within your spirit for more? The roar will always start with a groan. "Yet when holy lovers of God cry out to him with all their hearts, the Lord will hear them and come to rescue them from all their troubles" (Ps. 34:17 TPT). It is time to allow desperation to once again lead to the restoration of your roar and the roar He is longing to hear. Your awakening will cause others to hear a sound and come running to find freedom. Right now, God is looking for bold and courageous leaders who have a holy fear of the Lord to arise and stand firm. These are those who are not worried about losing their reputations or their standing but understand that they gain strength and purpose in God. You were rescued, revived, and restored for something greater than yourself. With great freedom and blessing comes great responsibility. God not only wants you to walk free of fear, but He also wants to see you rescue and revive both those around you and the next generation of freedom fighters.

Amos 3:8 says, "The lion has roared; who will not fear? The Lord God has spoken; who can but prophesy?" (MEV). It is time to restore your roar!

PAT SCHATZLINE
Evangelist and author
Remnant Ministries International

21

Burning for Revival

And the Lord has washed away the filth
of the daughters of Zion and cleansed the
bloodstains of Jerusalem by a Spirit of
justice and by a Spirit of burning.
—Isaiah 4:4 TPT

WHAT IF I TOLD YOU THAT YOU WERE CALLED TO BE A HIS-tory maker? That God wants to use you to make history with Him? I am convinced that the course of history is determined by the burning ones, the remnant. As we study history and the past moves of the Holy Spirit, we see a common factor—these burning ones were apprehended by the Burning One. We see illustrations of this throughout the Scriptures in the lives of Moses, Elijah, John the Baptist, and two men on the road to Emmaus. Let's take a look.

Moses' life at every turn was marked by the supernatural. As a baby he was providentially saved by Pharaoh's daughter. He was then raised in the house of Pharaoh and trained in all the culture of Egypt (see Acts 7:22). It was not uncommon for him to see the supernatural as we understand there were magicians who practiced witchcraft throughout Egypt. Fast-forward eighty years and we find Moses on the back side of the desert shepherding his father-in-law's sheep when everything suddenly changes. You see, when you come to the back side of the desert, where you think that God has completely forgotten about you, get ready for an encounter with the Burning One. We see this supernatural encounter in Exodus 3:2-3:

> *The angel of the Lord appeared to him in a blazing fire from the midst of a bush; and he looked, and behold, the bush was burning with fire, yet the bush was not consumed. So Moses said, "I must turn aside now and see this marvelous sight, why the bush is not burned up"* (NASB).

The moment that Moses turned aside and stepped toward the burning bush, he had an encounter with the Burning One that forever transformed his life. God came with His glory fire to purify Moses of all the Egyptian culture and raise him up as a deliverer of His people. God is manifesting this same glory fire now to come and burn us with His holy fire. We must first encounter Him so that He can purify and use us for His glory. All it takes is one man or woman who has been burned by God's presence to deliver nations, cities, and families.

Elijah was a man with a nature like ours (see James 5:17). From the Scriptures we do not know much concerning his early life. Yet we see him passionately burst onto the scene in First Kings 17 ready to retake the nation of Israel back for Yahweh. Elijah was burning with the Spirit of God so fervently that he could no longer tolerate the Baal worship and all that Jezebel had instituted in the nation. You and I know the story of him confronting all the false prophets of Jezebel and rebuilding the altar of the Lord. God supernaturally attested to what Elijah was doing on His behalf by sending fire from Heaven to consume his sacrifice. Like Elijah, God is calling for us to become a living sacrifice that is all consumed by His fire. We, as His burning ones in the earth, are coming to confront the forces of darkness in our land to change the course of history.

I think you are starting to see how history is in the hands of the burning ones—those upon whom the Spirit of Burning has come to blaze a trail of revival. Like John the Baptist, of whom Jesus testified, "John was a blazing, burning torch, and for a short time you basked in his light with great joy" (John 5:35 TPT). God is raising you and me up to be a burning torch in our generation. Together, on this journey, we will be like those Jesus encountered on the road to Emmaus:

> *Stunned, they looked at each other and said, "Why didn't we recognize it was him? Didn't our hearts burn with the flames of holy passion while we walked beside him? He unveiled for us such profound revelation from the Scriptures!"* (Luke 24:32 TPT)

Let's pray! Father, right now, impart the Spirit of burning to me. Set me on fire for revival! May every part of my being burn for Him in Jesus' name!

MYLES KILBY
The River Church
Savannah, Georgia

22

Be a Doer

THE HOLY SPIRIT IS SENDING AN AWAKENING THAT IS CAUS-
ing the sons and daughters of God to wake up and realize that,
having repented and received Jesus as Lord, it is no longer us
who live but *the actual Christ* who lives in us. We are going to
start believing not just with a head knowledge but with a heart
reality that as He is, so are we in this world (see 1 John 4:17).

Revival often begins with a personal invitation to respond
to the Holy Spirit tugging your heart to come closer. As we
open our hearts transparently in conversation with God in
humility, repentance, and faith, personal revival brings a reset
and reminder of the truth that God forgives us, restores us,
and wants to be Lord of every area of our lives. Then, filled
with the holy confidence that comes from knowing we are forgiven and that the same spirit that raised Christ from the dead
is upon us, our personal revival fire spills out and impacts the
world around us.

Understanding that we are new creations in Christ gives us
the confidence to manifest who Jesus is in our everyday lives.
"As he thinks in his heart, so is he" (Prov. 23:7). Instead of
thinking, *Well, I'm just a Christian. I've heard about healing.
I could give it a go,* it would be wonderful if we realized that

today it is no longer us who live but Christ—the same Christ who walked the earth and healed all who came to Him. We must remember the Bible teaches us to reckon ourselves dead. By the grace of God, we are alive to Him in Christ, anointed by the Holy Spirit, and we need to see us ourselves as new, not by our works but by His great goodness. As He is, so are we.

> *But be doers of the word, and not hearers only, deceiving yourselves. For if anyone is a hearer of the word and not a doer, he is like a man observing his natural face in a mirror; for he observes himself, goes away, and immediately forgets what kind of man he was. But he who looks into the perfect law of liberty and continues in it, and is not a forgetful hearer but a doer of the work, this one will be blessed in what he does* (James 1:22-25).

Have we forgotten what we look like? If we are not doing all the works of Jesus or if we're not doing all the things the Bible says we can do, it is not because we need to try harder, or we're bad people, or we're hypocrites, or we are somehow lacking in something. It is because we have forgotten what we look like. We have looked into the mirror of His Word, then walked away and thought, *Oh, I'll get there one day.* But if we look in the mirror of His Word and see Him, we discover what we look like. He is our mirror. Revival begins with revelation.

Let's remind ourselves what we look like. The Bible tells us in Second Corinthians 3:18, "But we all, with unveiled face, beholding as in a mirror the glory of the Lord, are being transformed into the same image from glory to glory, just as by the Spirit of the Lord," and, "God's power has given us everything we need for life and godliness, through our knowing the One who called us to his own glory and goodness" (2 Peter 1:3 CJB).

Second Peter 1:9 says that those of us who lack these things are shortsighted, even to blindness, and have forgotten that we were cleansed from our old sins. In other words, if we are lacking any of the virtues of the nature of God, the fruits of the Spirit, and the power of God in our everyday manifestations— it is because *we have forgotten that we have been cleansed of our past sins.* He took away our old life and gave us His life in exchange. That life is tangible. It is glistening life that we have to give away. It is the Word of life. A life of revival is a life of faith empowered by the daily revelation of who we are in Christ. The same Spirit who raised Christ from the dead lives in us and we can say, "Such as I have give I thee." Hallelujah!

KATHERINE RUONALA
Author, *Living in the Miraculous, Wilderness
to Wonders, Life with the Holy Spirit,
Speak Life, Supernatural Freedom*
Senior Leader, Glory City Church
Founder and facilitator, Australian Prophetic Council
www.katherineruonala.com

23

A Holy Dissatisfaction

I know your works, that you are neither cold nor
hot. I could wish you were cold or hot. So then,
because you are lukewarm, and neither cold
nor hot, I will vomit you out of My mouth.
—REVELATION 3:15-16

WHEN I WAS FIFTEEN, A SPITFIRE YOUTH DIRECTOR WALKED
into our conservative church and rocked my spiritual world.
He was an undercover Spirit-filled believer named John. I had
never been around anyone so in love with Jesus.

I remember riding around Lake Jackson with John when
the park was crowded with teenagers and families. John stuck
his head out the window and yelled, *"I love Jesus!"* loud enough
for the whole town to hear. I was mortified. As a shy, skinny
teenager, I sunk down in the seat, hoping no one saw me in
the car with this maniac, but I never forgot it. I never forgot
how John wasn't satisfied with people going on with their lives
while on their way to hell. He wasn't satisfied with singing
three verses and a chorus before half-listening to a sermon

and checking off your God list for one more week. He wasn't satisfied with being powerless and defeated.

He inspired in me a holy dissatisfaction that began in my teen years when I was exposed to an authentic representation of Jesus. I actually became upset with my denomination for denying the Holy Spirit's power to save, heal, and deliver today. I saw my first deliverance a couple of years later when John cast several demons out of a dear lady. The Scriptures were coming alive to me. More, Lord! I wanted more of His holy dissatisfaction.

In the Bible, revival was birthed out of a holy dissatisfaction with the status quo or religion-as-usual. As Israel became too familiar with God, not honoring His word, they would fall away. During the time of Hosea, Israel was outwardly enjoying a time of prosperity and growth, but inwardly moral corruption and spiritual adultery permeated the people. Hosea offered the possibility of salvation if only the nation would turn from idolatry back to God (see Hos. 14:1). His holy dissatisfaction was a catalyst that spread to the people and brought revival.

Similarly, we substitute our programs and methods for the fresh fire of the Holy Spirit; it's business as usual. Believers allow other gods to be erected in their lives until we are so far from the One True God.

For revival to manifest in our lives and churches, there has to be a holy dissatisfaction with how we do church. In fact, Christians must strongly consider leaving a church that teaches that the gifts of the Spirit are no longer for today. I did, and it made all the difference in my spiritual destiny!

Regrettably, some mainline churches have missed every great awakening in this nation, although they eventually benefited from the many souls brought into the Kingdom from these revivals.

The Church in revival is on the cutting edge of what God wants to do on the earth. In revival, we go from glory to glory, and it should never end. When God's Spirit shows up, manifestations of His power are evident to all. We see this clearly in Scripture, but many churches trust more in the devil to deceive than the Lord to lead us. We must teach the *whole* counsel of God concerning the Kingdom of God. Jesus came preaching the Kingdom of God, which encompasses salvation, healing, and deliverance. Too often, pastors either don't believe in the Kingdom message or they are afraid that the gifts and manifestations will offend someone. Revival in these types of churches will never happen unless they get a holy dissatisfaction and a new wineskin.

Revival is always birthed out of a prayer movement, and so from this holy dissatisfaction I've mentioned, we are driven to Second Chronicles 7:14: "If my people, which are called by my name, shall humble themselves, and pray, and seek my face, and turn from their wicked ways; then will I hear from heaven, and will forgive their sin, and will heal their land" (KJV).

I find myself being driven to spend more time in prayer— not just asking God for things, but repenting for my sins and the sins of the nation. Through praying and soaking in His presence, the Holy Spirit has the opportunity to show us things that are not pleasing to Him, things we missed before.

Personal holiness will always be a byproduct of time spent seeking God in prayer, time spent exploring our holy dissatisfaction. And our lives will be screaming *"I love Jesus!"* for a dying world to hear.

LOUIS JOHNSON
Senior pastor, Vine Church
Troy, Alabama

24

Kingdom Revival

KINGDOM REVIVAL! THAT IS WHAT WE NEED IN AMERICA AND in the nations of the earth. Many people have been praying, prophesying, and declaring for decades that America will experience another Great Awakening. I believe now is the time to see the manifestation of these prayers and declarations.

God is looking for one person to burn for Him in the place of prayer. This is how revival starts in a city or nation. There is no limit to what God can do with a person committed to prayer and fasting. Matthew 6:6 says, "But you, when you pray, go into your room, and when you have shut your door, pray to your Father who is in the secret place; and your Father who sees in secret will reward you openly." Personal revival begins in the secret place and prayer is the birthplace of revival. We become more like God as we spend time with Him in prayer and we begin to take on God's nature and His characteristics. Then we become carriers of glory and can spark Kingdom revival!

Early in my walk with the Lord, I was defined by this Scripture: "Now in the morning, having risen a long while before daylight, He went out and departed to a solitary place; and there He prayed" (Mark 1:35). Every day Jesus modeled

Kingdom living by rising early each morning and spending time in prayer with His Father. Jesus understood the importance of getting alone to hear from God. He knew that spending time in prayer was the only way He could accomplish everything His Father had called Him to accomplish. Years ago, I made a promise to myself, and to the Lord, that I would be a man who would be in the secret place of prayer every single day. The fruit of my life has been produced because of this commitment. God can accomplish anything with a person who has given their life to prayer in order to see the Kingdom manifested on the earth!

In Heaven, there are blueprints for everything. God has a specific plan for your life, family, business, ministry, and for the nations. The only way to access the plan of Heaven is through prayer! In Matthew 6:10, Jesus prays, "Your Kingdom come. Your will be done on earth as it is in heaven." When we come into agreement with that prayer and that proclamation, we are partnering with all of Heaven to see the Kingdom of God advance in the earth. Jesus is alive and He is at the right hand of the Father interceding for us. When we come into agreement with His prayers, we are crying out for everything in our lives to align with what Heaven is saying. As believers, it is important for us to partner with Jesus' prayers to see revival and awakening released into the earth.

Many people never reach their destiny because they have not committed themselves to hear from God. In prayer, God speaks to us and gives us direction for our lives. Psalm 32:8 says, "I will instruct you and teach you in the way you should go; I will guide you with My eye." The Holy Spirit wants to teach you and help you navigate your life. Without this instruction from the Lord, you can never hit your mark. However, as you listen to His instruction and allow the Lord to guide you, you will fulfill your God-given destiny.

God wants you to walk in the fullness of your purpose and destiny more than you do! This is why He gives us prophetic words and promises to help lead and guide us in our calling. Jesus Himself said in Luke 4:43, "I must preach the kingdom of God to the other cities also, because for this purpose I have been sent." Jesus knew He was sent to preach and teach the Kingdom of God. The Kingdom of God was manifested anywhere Jesus taught and people experienced Kingdom revival. The Lord needs each one of us to manifest our Kingdom assignment in the earth. This is the only way America and the nations will experience revival and awakening. We must be about the Father's business in this hour. America and the nations of the world need to be awakened and experience Kingdom revival, and you have a part to play for the Kingdom of God!

JOE JOE DAWSON
ROAR Apostolic Network
ROAR Church Texarkana
Joejoedawson.net

25

Prayer: The Prerequisite for Revival

JOHN WESLEY WAS ONCE ASKED HOW HE MANAGED TO GATHER such large crowds to listen to him preach. His response was immediate: "I set myself on fire and people come to watch me burn!" Where does that kind of fire come from? That kind of revival fire is ignited by the burning lampstand of fervent intercession.

What does a fire do? It warms and enlightens. It purifies. It empowers. A spiritual fire does the same things as a natural fire—it warms up a cold heart and makes it desire God. It releases the revelation like rays of light so that, suddenly, it's as if "the lights just came on." It burns sin out and brings cleansing to hearts and souls. And it releases new zeal and power into a believer's life. When we're praying for revival, we're praying for revival fire. We're praying for a firestorm.

Prayer is an absolute prerequisite for revival. It stems from a hunger and an intense desire for *change*. Something simply must change in the situation, because the situation is intolerable. Or—tell me if you have not experienced this yourself—it's more as if something must change in the situation, because the situation is just plain boring! You know what I mean.

You have gone along for some time, and nothing has seemed very exciting. Church just isn't quite meeting your needs. You can't figure out what your purpose is, and you're not sure the people around you know what theirs is either. You can't quite put your finger on what's wrong, but you get frustrated with it. In times like these, your heart and mouth can release grumbling and accusation—or prayer. If you want to get out of the doldrums and into revival, choose prayer. Prayer definitely changes things.

Another prerequisite for revival is networking. People begin to pull together in *unity*. They begin to pool their efforts and their prayers. They begin to cry out with one voice: "Lord, we need You! We are hungry for You. We are utterly dependent upon You." The relational work of networking results in progress toward unified prayer with an identifiable goal. Praying as a team gives feet to your restlessness and hope in the midst of your spiritual hunger.

Prayer and more prayer is the appropriate response to desperate times. Extreme prayer at all hours of the day and night is the only appropriate application of effort before, during, and after a time of revival from God. God wants to revive His people, wherever they may live. In other words, revival is *His* work, and the way we participate is to engage *Him* in all prayerfulness.

Charles Finney, who was known for his phenomenal evangelistic successes during the Second Great Awakening in the United States, had equally phenomenal prayer support behind the scenes. He is quoted as having said, "Revival is no more a miracle than a crop of wheat. Revival comes from Heaven when heroic souls enter the conflict determined to win or die—or if need be, to win and die."

Not just any kind of prayer will do. This kind of praying makes you sweat. It is hard work. It's often compared to the travail of childbirth. Leonard Ravenhill, a twentieth-century British revivalist, once said, "At God's counter there are no sale days, for the price for revival is ever the same—travail."

This kind of prayer will incur opposition. Persecution, opposition, and challenge are guaranteed. No advance of the Kingdom goes unchallenged; what you challenge will challenge you back. If you target individuals in prayer, persecution will come to you from individuals. If you target the Church in prayer, opposition will come from the Church. If you target the society around you, some segment of that society will fight back.

Therefore, you need even more fervency and even more of the Spirit of revival. Like those who have gone before you, you need to press forward, undaunted, linked arm in arm and spirit to spirit with your fellow intercessors, walking together through the conflict with other prayer warriors until victory is achieved. And then, after revival has come, you must support each other in the great work of stewarding the longed-for move of God.

JAMES GOLL
Author, prophet, and founder of
God Encounters Ministry

26

The Romans 11 Revival

"You can take a horse to the water but you can't make it drink." Steve Hill, the evangelist at the Brownsville revival, would often bellow, "But you can! You just need to salt its oats!"

As the deer pants for streams of water, so my soul pants for you (Psalm 42:1 NIV).

Our oats had been salted and we were thirsty. We listened, repented, laughed, cried, prayed, and interceded. Sometimes we'd just lie prostrate in His presence during times of worship when the anointing was so thick we dared not say a word. Oh, how we fell in love with Him. May the same happen to you!

We saw multiplied thousands lining up early mornings and waiting all day for the doors to open to hear a message of repentance and then run to the altar to give their lives to Jesus. People driving by would experience an overwhelming desire to turn in and attend while others traveled from across the globe to meet with Jesus. There was no advertising, no marketing, no social media or the internet. It was all God! It was supernatural.

Revival is no respecter of persons. From the lowest to the highest, ignorant to educated, aristocrat to commoner, God touches us all the same. We ran to the mercy seat unaware of personal differences, class, color, or creed. Once you have experienced revival, nothing else can satisfy. It will shake you and shape you! *It makes you shun sin and seek holiness.* No stone left unturned. Revival is our destination and we must get there at all costs.

Revival is life from the dead, and the greatest revival that will sweep the earth will happen when our Jewish brothers and sisters come to faith in Yeshua Messiah. This is in keeping with what the apostle Paul writes in Romans 11:11-15 concerning the Jewish people:

> *Did they stumble so as to fall beyond recovery? Not at all! Rather, because of their transgression, salvation has come to the Gentiles to make Israel envious. But if their transgression means riches for the world, and their loss means riches for the Gentiles, how much greater riches will their full inclusion bring. ...**For if their rejection brought reconciliation to the world, what will their acceptance be but life from the dead**?* (NIV)

There are multiplied thousands of Jews all around the world coming to faith in Yeshua but it's not enough. There are more than nine million Jews in Israel alone who do not know Jesus as Lord and Savior. Remember Paul's words—if their loss brought riches to the Gentiles and their transgression brought riches to the world, imagine what will happen when they get it right. Paul says it is *life from the dead!* It is because of the Jews that we have received the Gospel of Jesus Christ. It's time to return the blessing. It's time to pray for the salvation of God's chosen people. As I am writing this, GOD TV has recently launched the first ever Hebrew-speaking Christian cable television channel in Israel and we are praying that this historic, supernatural, and prophetic undertaking will result in reaping a huge harvest of souls. *Pray with us and let's believe to see all Israel saved!* In the meantime, may you also experience hunger and thirst for God like never before. May you burn with passion and may your life be set ablaze with His presence and power just like the hundreds of thousands who walked through those glorious doors in Pensacola Florida.

WARD SIMPSON
PRESIDENT AND CEO OF GOD TV

27

The Spirit of Awakening

*For this reason it says, "Awake, sleeper, and arise
from the dead, and Christ will shine on you."*
—EPHESIANS 5:14 NASB

And eye salve to anoint your eyes so that you may see.
—REVELATION 3:18 NASB

MAY WE CONTEND FOR THE SPIRIT OF AWAKENING TO BE
released to us both individually and corporately.

May we awaken to fresh and radical love.

May we awaken to the call of the Bridegroom.

May we awaken to intimacy and a first-love lifestyle.

The Father is raising up a prophetic generation to be
planted in Him. He is anointing our eyes to see, our ears to
hear, and our hearts to know. There is a release of spiritual
vision, gifts, and awakening! The Father is calling forth those
to teach, train, impart, and activate a prophetic people who
will arise in the earth and move with Him.

He is releasing fresh vision so that we can see Him clearly
in all of His glory. As we look ahead with unhindered vision,

we will become walking, breathing testimonies of revival. Once we have been awakened to see Him, we will burn with passion, calling others to live in the same unique place of intimacy. This is revival in motion! We burn in order to ignite others.

As our eyes are clarified to see with prophetic vision, we will discover the ways of the Father. We will move in sync with Him. We will not be ahead or behind, but in step with His plans on the earth. Prophetic people release the testimony of Jesus. They share the power and glory of the Resurrected One.

I believe that God wants to open your eyes today and release fresh vision for your next season. He wants to encounter you and release His mandate of awakening in your heart. He wants to bring you into a place of burning love and desire.

Prayer

Father, I thank You for the Spirit of Awakening. Wake me up to Your plans and desires. Wake me up to Your mandate in the earth. Release the Spirit of Awakening upon Your people, oh God. Release the Spirit of Awakening in our nation, in the name of Jesus. Amen.

I decree that I have eyes to see.

I walk in prophetic vision.

I see the plans of God.

I see the visions of the Lord.

I have prophetic dreams and visions.

I see the beauty and majesty of Jesus.

I see the plans and purposes of God.

I see with eyes of love and compassion for others.
I see God's heart for other people.
I see the nations caught up in revival.
I see the earth being consumed with the burning love of Jesus.
I see with heavenly vision.
I am seated with Jesus and therefore I see through His lens.
I have an aerial view.
My vision is expansive.
My eyes are anointed to see God's plans and purposes, in the name of Jesus. Amen.

RYAN LESTRANGE
Apostolic leader
Founder of TRIBE Apostolic Network
www.ryanlestrange.com

28

Holiness Today, Miracles Tomorrow

Then Joshua told the people, "Purify yourselves, for tomorrow the Lord will do great wonders among you."
—JOSHUA 3:5 NLT

REVIVAL BREEDS REVIVAL. I WAS BORN AGAIN IN THE 1990s, a time when movements such as the Argentine Revival, Toronto Blessing, Lakeland Outpouring, and Brownsville Revival were rocking the church. I was ruined for good. Throughout the entirety of my Christianity and subsequent ministry, I have been a revival junkie. As a teenager, my youth group in Georgia experienced revival. From 1999 to 2007, I lived in Chihuahua, Mexico as a missionary, and I was privileged to be a part of revival multiplying across that nation. From 2008 to 2014, my wife, Liz, and I were youth pastors in New Mexico, and our teens and young adults experienced a life-changing outpouring of the Holy Spirit. In 2014, with about twenty of those revived young adults, we moved to the Atlanta metro to plant Encounter Church, where one of our highest goals is, guess what—*revival!* So you see, revival breeds revival.

As far as I'm concerned, if we're not experiencing an outpouring of the Holy Spirit, what are we even doing? As the last days progress, we should be experiencing continuous, increasing outpouring because the heavens have been permanently open since the Day of Pentecost. I believe ongoing revival is God's will for the Church until we complete the task of making disciples of all nations.

When I was born again, I was automatically immersed into *discipleship*. I was taught God's Word and connected with leaders who, albeit imperfect, intentionally modeled the pursuit of a holy life. As a result of my introduction into Christianity, I can honestly say that after nearly 25 years, I have never even once considered turning back from following Jesus. Discipleship set the course of my life!

Discipleship is following Jesus and helping others follow Jesus. It is a never-ending learning process through which we become like Him. Through discipleship, we learn to go Jesus' way rather than our own way. It's a whole new way of thinking, seeing, hearing, feeling, wanting, talking, and treating people—a.k.a. *holiness!*

In Joshua 3:5, the leader of "the church," Joshua, was in essence speaking to his disciples when he said: "Purify yourselves, for tomorrow the Lord will do great wonders among you." In the next few chapters, we witness radical obedience. Not only do the people obey the command to abstain from impure behaviors; Joshua also proceeds to *circumcise* an entire new generation of Israelites before they move into enemy territory. Then, after their period of healing, Israel supernaturally defeats Jericho and makes their entrance into the Promised Land. What a *miracle!*

As we can see from Joshua's example, the pursuit of *purity* positions us to experience God's *power*. The daily pursuit of *holiness* prepares me for God to use my life in a *miraculous* way. Holiness today, miracles tomorrow!

For the New Testament believer, circumcision represents cutting away worldliness, impurity, ungodly habits, and questionable behavior. Circumcision is a picture of what the Spirit does in our hearts when we are born again, but it also is a picture of discipleship—giving up our life (flesh), taking up our cross (knife), and following Him (obedience).

People experience "the presence" in our church meetings, but are we teaching them to pay "the price" necessary to continue enjoying a lifestyle of His presence? What price? *Discipleship!*

In this new wave of revival, we must teach and model a life of holiness to Jesus' precious Church, so that together we can experience the greater works Jesus promised. Holiness today, miracles tomorrow!

HUNTER and LIZ HOWARD
Lead pastors, Encounter Church
Kennesaw, Georgia

29

Don't Take "No" for an Answer

I will not let You go unless You bless me!
—GENESIS 32:26

YOU WERE BORN INTO THE KINGDOM FOR SUCH A TIME AS this, to bring God's transformation to this generation! God is not limited by geography or the size of the congregation. My husband, Ray, and I pastor River of Destiny Church, located in a small town, population 500, in the middle of cornfields. John 1:46 says, "Can anything good come out of Nazareth?"

In June of 2003, I dreamt of a large room—so large that I couldn't see all the walls. It was white and very bright. In the center of the room was a large table in the shape of a cross. Many varieties of fruit and food were on the table. People were eating, talking, and laughing in an atmosphere that was full of life. Then, the scene changed to a map of the United States and South America. Lighted arrows from around the outside of the United States pointed to our location. I was awakened with an audible voice that said, "This is a focal point. People from all over the world will be coming here." How could this be? We have no restaurants, gas stations, hotels, or even a stoplight.

Soon after we started the church, I became very discouraged. I wanted to quit many times. We weren't growing. We struggled with only a handful of people. Living in a small community, as a Korean woman who can't speak English well, I felt I had three strikes against me before I had even started. I felt inadequate and unqualified but determined. I fasted forty days to seek God's will. After the fast, someone donated money toward our church building, then a building was given to us! The money we received renovated the building. When the Lord told us to start a church, I requested only one thing: "Lord, I will do whatever You ask; but if I ever have to worry about money, I'm done." The Lord has been faithful to His promise.

> *Instead, God chose things the world considers foolish in order to shame those who think they are wise. And he chose things that are powerless to shame those who are powerful. God chose things despised by the world, things counted as nothing at all, and used them to bring to nothing what the world considers important* (1 Corinthians 1:27-28 NLT).

This Scripture fits me perfectly! God doesn't choose the qualified; He qualifies the chosen. One time the Lord told me, "Yong, when I ask you to do something, even though you think it's impossible, I already put in you to do what I ask you to do. *If you do the possible, I will do the impossible!*" I decided that I will not limit God, and I will do everything He purposed for me to do!

After the dream, things got worse instead of better. The enemy tried to ruin our character, reputation, and finances so we would quit and not fulfill our God-given dream. During that dark season, the Lord said, "Yong, when you walk through the valley of the shadow of death, *don't even pause!* I am preparing a table before you while the enemy is watching. He thinks he's got you, but I am preparing you for an anointing."

Can a small church in Lostant, Illinois, shake and change the world? Our story is God's story.

My dream compelled me to pursue God's plan passionately. We went to church every day, praying and crying out to God for revival. One time, we fasted for 40 days and came together every night to pray. On day forty, we prayed all night. We are here today because we didn't give up. He is a rewarder of those who diligently seek Him.

We're still pursuing God's plan, and this dream is ever unfolding. It's been amazing to see international attendance for our church conferences and how the Lord is transforming lives. We believe that we are carriers of revival. I realize more than ever that God is the God of the impossible!

Do you have a promise from God, a prophetic word, or a dream? Don't ever give up! *Don't even pause!*

Pursue your dream! The Lord will fulfill His purpose for you!

YONG BRIERLY
Lead pastor, River of Destiny Church
Lostant, Illinois
www.riverofdestineychurch.com

30

Contending for Revival

Behold, I give to him My covenant of peace...
because he was zealous for his God, and made
atonement for the children of Israel.
—NUMBERS 25:12-13

IT WAS MAY OF 2009 WHEN EVERYTHING BEGAN TO SHIFT. I had been saved and filled with the Spirit for almost seven years—delivered from sin and a dark street life. The day I was saved, I heard an audible voice calling me to preach as I wept at the altar. In an instant, my life was drastically changed from darkness to light. Seven years later, I was a member, serving in the church where I had been saved, and I could feel God's fire burning hot within me.

One month before, my pastor announced that he would be leaving. The board approached me, asking if I would consider being the interim pastor until a permanent replacement could be found. In prayer, I heard the Spirit say, "Feed My sheep." By faith, I stepped in as interim pastor knowing nothing, except my God was able.

Revival Breakout

One month later, revival broke out. The Spirit of God began to move powerfully. Many were being saved, healed, delivered, and filled with the Spirit. In five months, the church had doubled in attendance, the giving was unprecedented—God was moving. The board approached me again, this time asking if I would become the lead pastor. I prayed and, once again, I heard the Spirit say, "Feed My sheep." I accepted and, ever since, our church has been in perpetual revival.

When people ask, "How do you keep such a spirit of revival?" My response is always the same. *We are always contending for it.*

Revival Killers and Contenders

Almost every week there is some kind of revival killer we have to face down. It has been that way since revival showed up, and from my experience, it always will be.

In Numbers 25, we find a story of contending. The children of Israel were experiencing a move of God—a revival. It didn't take long for the revival killer to show up. The people of God sinned and aroused the Lord's anger. Revival fire was at risk of dying out and leaving only yesterday's ashes.

A man who had no reverence for godly authority or His prophetic word defiantly paraded his Midianite woman before Moses and the leaders just before taking her into his tent to openly have sex with her. This was the deciding moment for the leaders of this revival. If this was allowed, the blessings would surely cease and the plague would continue. Faced with this, the people of God could give up or they could contend for their blessing.

In response, something powerful happened. A man named Phinehas retrieved his javelin, entered the tent, and killed the man and woman, stopping the plague. His willingness to contend for what God was pouring out brought blessing upon his future generations.

There's Always a Giant to Fight

Every time the Spirit moves, the enemy will send something to stop it—some kind of giant to extinguish the burning fires of revival. The difference between a quick burn and sustained revival fire is simply our willingness to contend for it. I've lost count of the number of tough decisions we've had to make to protect the outpouring of fire. It has caused us to be ridiculed, lied-on, and ostracized. However, we did it—not because we liked it, but because we were contending for revival.

Contending for Personal Revival

The same is true with our personal revival. As we contend, God will give us continual victory. However, we cannot back down in the face of the revival killer.

When God begins to pour holy fire on your life, giants will show up with demonic fire extinguishers. They take on different forms but have one agenda—to stop your revival. The difference between those who continue in personal revival and those who don't is simply the willingness to daily contend for it. We must never allow revival-killing giants to defiantly parade in the face of what God is doing. We must take up the javelin of intercession, praise, worship, and obedience. We must be zealous for the outpouring of the Lord and thus bless our generation and the generations to come.

PASTOR JEREMIAH HOSFORD
Abundant Life Church
Locust Grove, Georgia
Author of *21 Days to Overflow*

31

Embrace Your Place, Calling, Gifting

WE WELCOME REVIVAL IN OUR CHURCHES; JESUS SAID, "THE harvest truly is great, but the laborers are few; therefore pray the Lord of the harvest to send out laborers into His harvest" (Luke 10:2). We encourage all believers to not just attend church but also become the Church in manifesting His Kingdom in the power of the Holy Spirit. Jesus is seeking willing disciples to reveal Himself to the lost by powerful manifestations of the Holy Spirit:

> *The Spirit of the Lord is upon Me, because He has anointed Me to preach the gospel to the poor; He has sent Me to heal the brokenhearted, to proclaim liberty to the captives and recovery of sight to the blind, to set at liberty those who are oppressed; to proclaim the acceptable year of the Lord* (Luke 4:18-19).

We easily believe our Lord Jesus was given this divine commission to heal and deliver everyone oppressed of the devil. In Acts 10:38, this compassionate anointing is seen in action with Jesus "healing all who were oppressed by the devil." It is one thing to believe God anointed Jesus, but it is quite a stretch to believe we are anointed personally. Jesus has given encouragement to expect the impossible, the unimaginable, and to manifest the supernatural as He did. We read in First John 4:17, "as He [Jesus] is, so are we in this world." This identification with Christ must be spiritually discerned, because our natural minds are so aware of how unlike Jesus we are in the secrecy of our hearts. Know that God is greater than our condemning hearts; we are confident toward Him desiring to use us for His glory (see 1 John 3:20-21).

Jesus said, "Most assuredly, I say to you, he who believes in Me, the works that I do he will do also; and greater works than these he will do, because I go to My Father" (John 14:12). We marvel just reading about the miracles Jesus did, but believing we personally could do those works and even greater is overwhelming to our minds. We must accept our personal mandates to manifest Jesus' Kingdom as His disciples. In Mark 9:23, Jesus said, "If you can believe, all things are possible to him who believes." We all believe Jesus said that, but can we believe He really meant us?

We are immersed in an awareness of our "Christian celebrities" through television, radio, books, and magazines. Multitudes of believers attend large events to witness those "anointed of God" on stage. As spectator believers, we feel spiritually not enough to be used by God. We easily defer all opportunities to minister to the successful vessels of God. My concern is too many of us believe the anointing is only for God's special, chosen few. Ask the Holy Spirit to reveal your "fitly joined" place in supplying ministry to the Body of Christ (Eph. 4:16).

We know we are Holy Spirit filled; why would we doubt that the indwelling Holy Spirit, who raised Jesus from the dead, would work through us? Let's ask Him to reveal any hindering strongholds that so easily beset us (see Heb. 12:1). Instead of resisting His Spirit's promptings, we must press onward in strongly desiring the best gifts to glorify God. Declare, "Here am I, Lord, please use me!"

Being used in supernatural healings and deliverances is naturally outside of the scope of our natural minds; we easily avoid ministry opportunities. We should become aware when we avoid opportunities to glorify God. Doubt your doubts, forsake your fears, and embrace your God-given faith as a disciple of Christ. "God is able to do much more than we ask or think through His power working in us" (Eph. 3:20 NLV). Decide to take a quantum leap of faith toward your true potential for God's glory. Supernatural power already resides in us; it doesn't have to be prayerfully imported from Heaven. There is the ever-present power of the Holy Spirit desiring to work in us and through us! Seize every opportunity set before you.

MIKE MILLÉ
White Dove Fellowship
Harvey, Louisiana
www.whitedove.org

32

The Greatest Moments in History

PRACTICE IS OVER! THOSE WERE THE WORDS WE LONGED TO hear being shouted from our coach. Yet as a 14-year-old team handball player, hearing that led to my feeling a sudden seriousness and apprehension. Practice being over only meant that sooner than later, ready or not, it would soon be game time.

Our team had advanced to play in the southern regionals in Mineral Wells, Texas. On the line was a once-in-a-lifetime opportunity to qualify for the national championships in San Antonio.

As the game approached, I wondered—was I ready? Did I have what it takes to compete at a championship level and against the best my sport had to offer? Did I have it within me and could I rise to the occasion and challenge before me?

The night before the game, everyone went to the local amusement park but me. All I could think about was the game the next morning. This was my chance, and I did not want this opportunity to pass me by. I stayed behind and went to bed dreaming of what possibly could be.

On paper we did not stand a chance against the team we were matched against. They were larger, faster, and much more athletic. Yet when the final buzzer sounded, to everyone's amazement we were on top and would soon be on our way to the Alamo and San Antonio.

There has never been a time like right now on the earth. Nor has there ever been anyone exactly like you. These are the times the church has been waiting for and will discover she has been prepared for. The greatest opportunity to see the Kingdom of God come and His will done on earth as it is in Heaven is at hand.

> *For God may speak in one way, or in another, yet man does not perceive it. In a dream, in a vision of the night, when deep sleep falls upon men...then He open the ears of men, and seals their instruction* (Job 33:14-16).

Years later in a dream, I was walking through the middle of a massive crowd of people in a large open field. I knew that when I arrived at the stage on the other side of the field, I would have to address the people.

I could see in their eyes how they were desperate to hear a word that would give them hope. All along the journey while walking through the crowd, I kept asking God to give me something to say that would be from Him and what was most needed for that hour.

After arriving, I immediately walked onto the stage and up to the mic. Then out of my mouth came these words: "This is not the greatest time in the last decade. It's not the greatest time in a lifetime nor even a generation. These are the greatest days in all of history." The dream ended.

Jesus made it clear His disciples did not *choose Him* but rather He *choose them*. And in His choosing them He *appointed them* (see John 15:16). To *appoint* can mean *to place* or, to put it another way, *get them into their position.*

In considering these times, would a coach send his team to face the challenges of a championship game unprepared? If he wants to win and keep his job he would not. Likewise, would Jesus who loves His bride and has invested so much into her send her onto the field and into the final hours of this age unprepared or out of position? Absolutely not!

In the days to come it will not be about us. These times are all about the Lord's faithfulness to get us ready and in position for what will be *the greatest moments in all of history.*

Regardless of your circumstances and what you perceive as limitations, you were made for this moment!

The greatest moments in history are still to come.

> *Let us hold fast the confession of our faith without wavering, for He who promised is faithful* (Hebrews 10:23).

Dr. David White
Pastor, The Gathering Church
Moravian Falls, North Carolina

33

Press through the Wall

WHAT A BLESSING IT IS TO BE FILLED WITH THE HOLY GHOST and fire.

I want to talk to you about the blood covenant of the Lord Jesus, fasting, and prayer. I pray that your mind, body, and spirit be held complete in the Holy Ghost for the coming of the Lord Jesus Christ.

I want to bless you and encourage you. We know the world is going through some very difficult times, but I want to go on record and say Jesus is King! This means we, as God's children, we don't bend to the difficulty. And we don't submit to the lies of the devil. We don't fret and worry about our circumstances or our surroundings. What we do is call upon the Lord Jesus with prayer and fasting, with total submission of our bodies and our minds.

I just completed my forty-seventh marathon; the weather was hot, in fact, the hottest day of the year. The first 22 miles were a joy, but then came the work. Those who run call it "a wall." I hit the "running wall." It was difficult to push ahead. Just like in running, life is full of walls. Everything will be fine and then you come up against a wall. You have to press through that wall. I told the people I was running with, "I am not going to submit to my surroundings. I am going to submit to the goal; the goal is to complete the marathon." I stayed with it and finished the run. I was successful.

Right now, I bless you to be successful in your life and your endeavors. Running a marathon to me is like the Gospel—you have to train for it, you have to prepare for it, you have to put your spirit into it, your mind, your soul, your body, all of it. If you don't, you won't complete the task.

Paul was about to hit his own wall when he said:

> And see, now I go bound in the spirit to Jerusalem, not knowing the things that will happen to me there, except that the Holy Spirit testifies in every city, saying that chains and tribulations await me. But none of these things move me; nor do I count my life dear to myself, so that I may finish my race with joy, and the ministry which I received from the Lord Jesus, to testify to the gospel of the grace of God (Acts 20:22-24).

I want you to receive the strength of the Lord, the blessing of the Gospel that Christ Jesus empowers us and makes us ready and makes us equal to anything that is around us. He infuses us with energy and power to do things even in difficult times.

As for me and my house, we will serve the Lord because Jesus is King. I am not willing to submit to any power of darkness. I believe the Word of God is powerful, sharper than any two-edged sword, dividing asunder the soul and spirit. I believe we are baptized with Holy Ghost and fire and we can overcome through prayer and fasting. Fasting is difficult and it afflicts the soul, but we can do these things for the Holy Ghost. Other people may draw back from it, but we will not. The blood of Jesus is our answer; the Holy Ghost fire, the Word of God, which is alive and full of power, will see us through.

Don't forget, as a believer you can suppress, take away, remove, and destroy the works of the enemy by the blood covenant of the Lord Jesus Christ.

Take the time to seek the Lord, be strong and empowered. With your union with the Lord Jesus, draw strength and encouragement from the Holy Ghost and the fire of God. It's your choice—focus on His mercy and His goodness and His grace. Let Jesus be King and Lord in your life.

DAVID HOGAN
Missionary and international evangelist

34

Bars of Your Gates

The Lord takes pleasure in those who fear Him, in those who hope in His mercy. Praise the Lord, O Jerusalem! Praise your God, O Zion! For He has strengthened the bars of your gates; He has blessed your children within you. He makes peace in your borders, and fills you with the finest wheat.

—PSALM 147:11-14

A NUMBER OF YEARS AGO I WAS ASKED TO BE AN ADULT COUN-selor at a youth camp. It was an amazing experience—truly a revival, as God moved in a mighty way with many young people giving their lives to Jesus. The following year I returned as a camp counselor and many of the youth from the previous year had returned as well. As the opening evening of camp began, an opportunity was given for the youth to share their testimonies. One by one, young people came to the micro-phone and instead of sharing the joy of their salvation and the power of the Holy Spirit in their lives, they shared of failed dreams, backslidden lives, sinful behavior, of guilt and shame, etc. They may have gone home with a "new touch," but when they got home they still "touched" everything around them that adversely affected their spiritual life.

Psalm 147 is a psalm of praise to God. David is thanking God for the many things He does for His people and for Jerusalem, but what spoke to me in this psalm was verse 13. If we are to discover and remain in the presence of Jesus, verse 13 is key: "for God strengthens the bars of your gates." David's direct reference is to the city of God, to Jerusalem, but there is a deeper truth as well.

Those young people at camp were truly touched by Jesus, but when they returned home they did not "strengthen the bars of their gates" against sin, against the world, against the many things that seek to rob us of the joy of our salvation and the fullness of the Spirit-filled life. Revival does not end when someone makes a decision for Jesus or when a cold and lifeless Christian comes back to life. Revival is renewal and renewal can only take place as we daily keep distance from the things around us that are trying to steal our peace with God—trying to hide God's presence from us.

Are the "bars of your gates" strong? Are they strong enough for you to resist the enemy, to not allow sin to reign in your life? A gate has two purposes—to keep in and to keep out. When one or more of the bars of a gate are weakened then what is in—the love, peace, and joy of Jesus—can be easily attacked by what is out—sin, failure, and the things of the world. Listen to verses 12 and 13: "Extol the Lord, Jerusalem; praise your God, Zion. He strengthens the bars of your gates and *blesses your people within you*" (NIV).

First, we note that it is God who strengthens our gates. We are powerless without the help, the protection of God. He is our city of refuge and He has given us bars to strengthen our gates—prayer, the Word of God, worship, etc. The spiritual disciplines in our life are the bars that God provides to keep us safe in His presence regardless of what is on the outside trying to get in. When we allow God to strengthen the bars of our gates, we experience His blessings. But note verse 14—God also "grants peace to your borders" (NIV). The Hebrew word for *peace* is *shalom*. *Shalom* is commonly used in Hebrew today as a greeting—much like *hello*, but the word has a deeper meaning. *Shalom* is also used to express wholeness. Thus, when we offer a greeting of shalom, it is deeper than just hello—we are also wishing that person complete wholeness.

When the bars of our gates are strong and fortified by the spiritual disciplines God has given us, then truly we can experience shalom—complete wholeness. Those young people at camp had a touch from God, but they didn't allow God to strengthen the bars of their gates, so when they returned home the enemy crawled through the hole and looted—took from them what God had done. Let us "strengthen the bars of our gates" in the name and authority of Jesus! For we are more than conquerors through Him who loved us!

DENNIS WALLACE
Evangelist, mentor, and revivalist
Arlington, Kansas

35

He Knows My Name

But now, thus says the Lord, who created you,
O Jacob, and He who formed you, O Israel:
"Fear not, for I have redeemed you; I have
called you by your name; You are Mine."
—Isaiah 43:1

Only you and the Creator know the places deep within your soul where darkness and sin linger. Those areas where you desperately desire to be completely set free but wonder if that's a fantasy. Can those ugly places inside just vanish or be erased? Is that reality to have such high hopes?

As I sat among hundreds of women at the North Georgia Revival Women's Conference waiting to encounter God in the baptismal waters, I whispered in my spirit, "God, heal me." I really didn't believe He was listening. Suddenly, a voice came over the microphone; the pastor stopped baptizing and asked, "Is there a Linda here?"

Time stood still. It was surreal.

Out of hundreds, He called *me* by name. God heard my desperate cry.

I sprang to my feet and ran to the alter waving my hands, overtaken by the tangible presence of the Almighty God. As tears streamed down my face, I raised my hands toward Heaven and met the Lord face to face. With one look, He instantly cleansed me from a lifetime of guilt, shame, rejection, and unworthiness. The weight of His glory consumed every fiber of my being as I fell to the floor. Trembling from head to toe, His fire burned up generations of sin within me.

Never have I felt so free, light, loved, special, and chosen. The Lord called me by name to give me a new identity, to exchange my sin and failure for His love and healing, my regrets and misery for His grace and mercy. He revived my soul.

For days after, my body physically trembled. The weight of God's presence remained. One encounter changed the trajectory of my life forever.

Experiencing God's tangible presence brings tremendous power, beauty, and intimacy. Yet something greater follows a radical touch of God. We must live it out. Living out revival every single day of life is our commission. Revival is an awakening to God's presence that propels us to live different than before.

But, how do we carry revival—His presence—into everyday, ordinary living when we don't feel the weight of His glory by the trembling from within, a burning sensation on our skin, or electricity running down the spine? As a Christian life coach, I often refer others to read the chapter "Just Live Today" from my book *Worthy of a Miracle* as a guide in stewarding God's presence. I wrote this book after surviving cancer and being in a coma on life support during the 2009 swine flu pandemic.

Excerpt from Worthy of a Miracle

When I was diagnosed with cancer and was afraid I was going to die, I wanted my time back. I wanted to undo the days I'd let slip through my hands… the slow and sweet moments with my husband, and the simple silly moments with my daughter. I would sit on my front porch swing with the sinking feeling (the new reality!) that I only had that very hour, that very day. I could not go backward, and I was not guaranteed a future. I just had today. Looking back, I am finally aware of what a tremendous gift it was to recognize that all I had was that single moment. You see, every twenty-four hours is a gift—a "present" we are encouraged to accept. We have the choice to receive it and make it count. It's impossible to dwell in the past or the future if you remember you are in the presence of…in the present with…Jesus.

Dear reader, God is calling you by name into His loving presence. He's bringing you back from captivity and restoring your heart. He is reviving your soul. God lives outside time and space, which means you too can experience His tangible touch of revival. Physically raise your hands and receive Him in this very moment. Revival is here—right where you are sitting. Encounter Jesus like never before. He loves you. He sees you. He knows your name.

LINDA KUHAR
Certified Life Coach, Center for
Credentialing and Education
Certified Human Behavior Consultant
Author and speaker
www.lindakuhar.com.

36

Unbreakable Unity

AS PLANTS NEED SUNLIGHT AND AIR TO SURVIVE AND THRIVE, so true, genuine revival needs unity and humility to be sustained. Many people and churches have received a "touch" or "move" of God over the years, but it was short-lived.

As we study revivals in the past, we quickly learn that pride and disunity have brought many genuine moves of God to a screeching halt. Why is that? I personally believe it's because God cannot (will not) continually move in an atmosphere that He says He rejects. James 4:6 says that God opposes the proud, but gives grace to the humble. Disunity is always the fruit of pride—"only by pride cometh contention" (Prov. 13:10 KJV).

When we walk in pride, disunity, and division, God opposes us and revival seems to never happen or quickly dissipates.

However, when we humble ourselves, choose to forgive, and overlook offenses, God's influence in our lives is amplified, enabling us to be Christlike, have a Kingdom mindset, and walk in unity. Then, bam! Blessings, grace, mercy, power, and anointing overflow in your life creating, first of all, a personal revival, then making you a carrier of revival.

As Psalm 133 alludes, when people walk together in unity, there is an anointing released (*oil flowing from Aaron's beard*), and in the place of unity God *commands* a blessing. Who does not want to walk in the commanded blessing of God?

I'm sure our story is the same as many others. After all, human nature is human nature. We were going through a trying time in our local church and ministry. We had people who were on the outs with each other. There were some boiling points and the relational pot was about to tip in different areas. But God! Through the North Georgia Revival and what turned into the Southeast Louisiana revival, the presence of God touched people's lives and hearts. What could have been damaging and destructive became a beautiful blessing. When you choose humility and unity, the smile of God shines on your life and ministry.

Wherever you are today in your pursuit of revival, make sure you choose humility and unity as you move forward. A good pattern to follow is found in Colossians 3.

> *Therefore, as God's chosen people, holy and dearly loved, clothe yourselves with compassion, kindness, humility, gentleness and patience* (Colossians 3:12 NIV).

So ask yourself—am I walking in humility? Am I being compassionate and patient with people, even those with whom I might not see eye to eye?

> *Bear with each other and forgive one another if any of you has a grievance against someone. Forgive as the Lord forgave you* (Colossians 3:13 NIV).

"Bear with each other" carries the meaning of continuing to bear even after going through the needed course of action.

Are we bearing with those around us? Are we forgiving as the Lord forgave us? Think of all the things He has forgiven you for.

And over all these virtues put on love, which binds them all together in perfect unity (Colossians 3:14 NIV).

Here we see the word *unity* again! As we decide to put on love, it binds together all of the other characteristics in perfect unity!

Go for it! Be daring! Be courageous! Be humble! Forgive today, bear with your brothers and sisters today, be compassionate and watch yourself turn into a vessel of revival.

After all, one of Jesus' last prayers was that we would be one as He and the Father are One.

MERVIN STROTHER
Cornerstone Church
Amite, Louisiana

37

Brokenness

I long to drink of you, O God, drinking deeply from
the streams of pleasure flowing from your presence.
My longings overwhelm me for more of you! My soul
thirsts, pants, and longs for the living God. I want to
come and see the face of God. Day and night my tears
keep falling and my heart keeps crying for your help.
—PSALM 42:1-3 TPT

ONE OF THE GREATEST PRINCIPLES OF SPIRITUAL AWAKENING
is simply spiritual hunger! David's spiritual hunger for God
was marked by a constant yearning and desperation that was
expressed through weeping and lamenting. He wanted to just
drink from fountains of His presence, and he did. Brokenness
literally attracts the presence of God. Brokenness and contriteness are fountains of pleasure to God, but His presence
is a fountain of pleasure for *us!* There is a one-to-one corre-
spondence between brokenness and experiencing more of
the presence of God; this is a great exchange! God's appetite
is satiated by our brokenness, but *our* appetite is satiated by
His presence! As our souls are broken and poured out before

the Lord in repentance, it draws Him nearer to us, causing His presence to *flood our soul.* As we are filled with more of His presence, we are satisfied and our spirits break even more in His presence. It is a revolving door. David said he was so broken simply because he so wanted more of God's presence that he became overwhelmed. He said he was wheezing and gasping and panting like a dehydrated deer in search of water, his very soul desperate for the living God! He said his desire was just to see God face to face—this literally means he had no agenda except experiencing more of the presence and person of God! He wanted intimacy with the Lord. Then, he says, day and night his tears kept falling!

When I speak of spiritual hunger, it's not simply referring to crying or being emotional. This is more about having such a deep experience with God that it takes you to an emotional place. This is coming before God pouring out your heart and being afflicted in your soul. Like the woman with the alabaster box (see Luke 7:37), a shattered heart or an afflicted soul is one of the lowliest positions that display extreme humility and meekness. It's a cry for mercy and shows complete dependence upon God for help. Sometimes people may think that we only assume this position of desperation when we are in trouble or have an urgent prayer request. However, this should always be the daily positioning of our hearts, as believers, toward the Lord. Every. Single. Day. There must be a complete reliance on God, a brokenness toward God, and a yearning for the presence of God.

Our hearts should be like putty in the presence of God, filled with tenderness, desperation, hunger, gratitude, repentance, and remorse! We cannot have a lackadaisical attitude toward God! This should be our daily posturing in prayer, our daily posturing in worship, and our daily posturing in fasting. There should be such a deep yearning for God that you will not stop pursuing until you are completely satisfied and filled with His presence. Once you reach that satisfaction, new hunger arises, and God will continue to fill you up again and again as He pours out His Spirit without measure! Where deep hunger, brokenness, contriteness, and prayer are present, revival is not far off!

Prayer

I want to experience this deliciousness of overflowing with Your presence, God. Today, just as David prayed to experience fountains of Your presence. I ask You, Lord, to create in me a heart filled with spiritual hunger that I may experience those same rivers of living water—wells of life springing up on the inside of my soul! Like David, posture my heart toward You and prepare me for spiritual awakening!

PASTOR DERRICK M. SNODGRASS, JR.
Spiritual Prosperity Enrichment Center (S.P.E.C.)
Indianapolis, Indiana

38

Revival Is Not a Thing

Draw near to God and He will draw near to you.
—JAMES 4:8

THERE ARE GOD-ORDAINED MOMENTS THAT PRESENT THEM-selves throughout life. These experiences and encounters become pivotal junctures along your spiritual journey that forever mark you. When they come, seize them! One of those came for me unexpectedly during a conversation with Evangelist Steve Hill. Steve was the evangelist during a five-year-long historic outpouring that began in 1995 in Pensacola, Florida. Three and a half million people came through the doors during that move of God, and more than 100,000 salvations were recorded at the altar. It truly was a historic revival.

I was honored to work with Steve for fifteen years after that revival. During that time, we enjoyed many candid conversations. On this particular occasion, Steve brought up an article from a mutual friend that had recently been published in a major Christian magazine. Our friend shared his experience during the revival and the effect it had on his life. Steve shared how proud he was of this minister and the way he was being used in the Kingdom. However, I could tell there was also something that bothered him. So I asked.

Steve leaned back and said, "It's the way he wrote about revival. He said it was a wonderful season in his life, but like all seasons, it came to an end."

He continued, "That's what people do—they turn revival into a thing. They give it a beginning and an end—they book-end it. That way they can pick it up, enjoy it for a while, and then when they are done, close the book, put it on the shelf, and move on to the next thing."

Steve looked directly at me and with his unmistakable bold voice said, "Daniel, revival is God. How do you bookend God? How do you put God on a shelf and walk away? This is why revival has never ended for me. I've never treated revival as a thing!"

That day, Steve gave the best definition for revival and a secret for sustaining it.

When you think of revival, how do you define it? If you had asked me before that day, I might have talked about salvations, signs, wonders, miracles, crowded churches, extended meetings, and transformed cities. In other words, what I had experienced in my past. All these are wonderful things, but not one of them is revival. These come as a consequence of revival, but they themselves are not revival. True revival is far greater than that.

Revival is not some "thing" to be pursued; it is some "One" we pursue.

Revival is God's arrival! It comes when the eternal, all-consuming presence of the Lord walks into the room. It is when the King of kings enters a church or community and is allowed to inhabit His throne with absolute authority. It is the moment when you become fully alive in God and He becomes fully alive in you. That, my friend, is something altogether different from a season of extended church services!

James 4:8 says to "Draw near to God and He will draw near to you." This is an invitation to anyone who desires authentic revival. It is a reminder that revival does not come to a place but a position. When we make the conscious choice to place ourselves in closer proximity to Him, He promises to do the same. This is an unending, relational pursuit through which we are filled with His life. As long as we remain in Him, revival never ends.

Today is a perfect opportunity for one of those pivotal moments to find you. Stop chasing after revival as if it is something to experience, and start pursuing the One who wants to encounter you. I promise if you'll draw closer to Him, He will come closer to you.

Pastor Daniel K. Norris
Grace World Outreach Church
Author, *Trail of Fire* and *Receptivity*

39

The Greater Glory Has Started!

W E ARE LIVING IN THE SEASON OF THE *GREATER GLORY*. Romans 9:4 says the glory "belongs" to the Jewish people. A major outpouring of this glory occurred on Pentecost 2,000 years ago. Then a ragtag army of Jews from Israel took this glory to the Gentiles. Now we are at the time of the greater glory. Once more God will pour out His glory on the Jewish people in Israel to ignite the greatest revival in history:

> *Arise, Jerusalem! Let your light shine for all to see. For the glory of the Lord rises to shine on you. Darkness as black as night covers all the nations of the earth, but the glory of the Lord rises and appears over you. All nations will come to your light* (Isaiah 60:1-3 NLT).

Why do I call this the greater glory? Because Haggai 2:9 describes it as greater than the glory in the first Temple: "The *glory* of this *latter* house will be *greater* than the *former*, says the Lord of Hosts" (MEV).

What is the purpose of this greater glory being poured out on Israel? The same reason as before—to evangelize the Gentile:

Thus says the Lord of Hosts: In those days ten men from every language of the nations will take hold of the garment of a Jew, saying, "Let us go with you, for we have heard that God is with you" (Zechariah 8:23 MEV).

The greater glory will trigger the greatest Jewish revival in history. "To the Jew first" has always been God's pattern (Rom. 1:16 MEV). Then the Jewish believers will trigger the greatest Gentile revival in history.

God's passion is for *all* to be saved. First Timothy 2:3-4 says, "God our Savior...desires *all* men to be saved and to come to the knowledge of the truth" (MEV). This greater glory is God's last effort to evangelize the world. Sadly, not all will accept this mercy, but I see entire cities and even countries being saved!

This greater glory will be like no other we have seen in history. Paul says the restoration of Jewish people to the Body of Messiah will release resurrection power. In Romans 11, Paul writes:

So, am I saying that Israel stumbled so badly that they will never get back up? Certainly not! Rather, it was because of their stumble that salvation now extends to all the non-Jewish people, in order to make Israel jealous and desire the very things that God has freely given them. So if all the world is being greatly enriched through their failure, and through their fall great spiritual wealth is given to the non-Jewish people, imagine how much more [great spiritual wealth] *will Israel's awakening bring to us all! For if their temporary rejection released the reconciling power of grace into the world, what will happen when Israel is reinstated and reconciled to God? It will unleash resurrection power* [life from the dead] *throughout the whole earth!* (Romans 11:11-12,15 TPT)

This greater glory has started, but we haven't seen anything yet! Soon we will see the greater glory released like the trickle of water coming out of the Temple in Jerusalem that becomes a mighty river of God's greater glory (see Ezek. 47). I love the fact that in Ezekiel 47:9:

Every living creature...wherever the rivers go, will live. And there shall be a very great multitude of fish [symbolic of souls]...*Thus everything shall live **wherever** the river comes* (MEV).

What is the best way to be a carrier of this glory? *Do not seek the glory!* Instead, *seek the Lord* while He may be found. The glory will be an automatic result from the intimacy you develop with God.

What will this release of the greater glory look like? I see a time coming shortly when football stadiums will no longer be used for sporting events. Instead, they will be used to worship God. Our church buildings will not be large enough for all the new believers. Classrooms in colleges, high schools, and elementary schools will be invaded by the presence of God. The mushroom of the glory cloud will hang over entire cities. People will weep and repent and whole cities will come to Jesus.

My vision is big. But it doesn't catch God by surprise. Our God is *big!*

SID ROTH
Host, *It's Supernatural!* television

40

A Desire for More

On the last day, that great day of the feast, Jesus
stood and cried out, saying, "If anyone thirsts,
let him come to Me and drink. He who believes
in Me, as the Scripture has said, out of his heart
will flow rivers of living water." But this He spoke
concerning the Spirit, whom those believing in
Him would receive; for the Holy Spirit was not
yet given, because Jesus was not yet glorified.
—JOHN 7:37-39

"YOU WILL FEEL SOMETHING COMING FORTH OUT OF YOUR belly." These are the words that were spoken to me on February 22, 1998 at 2:15 a.m. by a Spirit-filled man who led me into the baptism of the Holy Spirit. As he and other men prayed with me, I encountered the Holy Spirit in a way I had never experienced before. This promise of the Holy Spirit spoken by Jesus Christ Himself became a reality to me. As I lay in the floor under the power of God, I wept and rejoiced as I felt the warm embrace of Jesus Christ Himself! A love for God and others exploded in my heart! My life has been forever changed as this passion for God continues to increase and intensify through the years!

Beyond Tradition

My spiritual background was different from the fresh, reviving encounter with the Holy Spirit I had on February 22, 1998. I had served as a denominational preacher and pastor for five and a half years. My denomination did not believe in the baptism of the Holy Spirit or the gifts of the Spirit (especially speaking in tongues). Although that was the environment and atmosphere I was typically in, there was a deep desire and hunger for more of the things of God! This is what true revival and spiritual awakening is. It is a drawing of the Holy Spirit upon a person where nothing else matters except a fully surrendered life to our heavenly Father. When Jesus baptized me in the Holy Spirit, all my doubts of this experience were erased as I finally knew this wonderful and glorious Holy Spirit baptism was real and available—even beyond my former spiritual traditions.

Out of Your Comfort Zone

A desire for more of God will pull you out of your comfort zones. Most all of us are creatures of habit and feel secure staying within the confines of our comfort zones. However, when our need and desire for God becomes greater than the security of our comfort zone, miracles and healings can occur. In Matthew 9:18-22, a woman with a flow of blood for twelve years pressed through the crowd of people surrounding Jesus and touched the hem of His garment. When she did this, she was immediately healed. Her healing came as a result of her desire to push through the borders and limitations to which she was confined.

According to Leviticus 15, a woman with her condition was considered unclean and everything that came in contact with her was also considered unclean. Therefore, this woman was a social outcast for many years. Her moment of breakthrough came when she realized that Jesus was her only hope. She said within herself, "If only I may touch His garment, I shall be made well." Her willingness to risk public embarrassment, criticism, and disappointment definitely took her out of her comfort zone, but it brought about a life-altering moment as Jesus responded to her by saying, "Be of good cheer, daughter; your faith has made you well." I have witnessed depression lifted from people, fear eradicated, addictions overcome, marriages restored, cancers disappear, and deaf ears open as a result of people stepping out of their comfort zones in complete trust and faith in God.

Communion Daily

I have found that true revival always begins with a spiritual awakening within an individual. As revival has taken place within my life, the Lord has given me a key that has personally kept the fire of the Holy Spirit burning within me daily. This key is partaking of communion daily. Communion is a springboard into intimacy with Jesus. As I take of the body and blood of our Lord Jesus Christ through communion, not only am I remembering the covenant that I have with Him, but I bring Him into my personal, present life. In doing this, I am able to fellowship and commune with Him.

Conclusion

No matter where you are on your spiritual journey, continue to have a desire for more of the things of God. This desire will take you beyond your traditions, out of your comfort zone, and into a life of communing with Jesus daily! May the fire of the Holy Spirit continue to burn in you as you pursue Him!

ROBBIE MATHIS
Lead pastor, Freedom Tabernacle
Cumming, Georgia

41

Essentials of Revival

The thief cometh not, but for to steal, and to kill,
and to destroy: I am come that they might have life,
and that they might have it more abundantly.
—John 10:10 KJV

Knowing my interior world isn't matching up with my exterior reality was very exhausting and disappointing. The constant struggle of doing my absolute best day in and day out to live a victorious Christian life was wearing me down to the ground. I was constantly questioning the very existence of my faith and everything I said I believed in. Is Jesus' resurrection really my resurrection? Do I really have power and authority over sin in my life? Am I really more than a conqueror? Is a victorious life really for me? Is it possible to experience life and life more abundantly every day? If so, why isn't this my reality? Why am I not experiencing the life Jesus came to freely give me?

I operated more like a failure most days than I did a conqueror. The feeling of living the life of an imposter haunted me every day of my life, and it seemed as though I could never escape it no matter how hard I tried. Yes, there were some days I functioned as an overcomer, but mostly I was filled with defeat and disappointment. Laying my head down at night knowing deep inside something was wrong, something was missing in my Christian life drove me to cry out to God for answers. I had finally come to an end of this continuous torture of being a failure, of never measuring up to the life Jesus came to impart to me.

After crying out to God and asking, "Why am I not experiencing the abundant life? Why am I not living in a constant state of revival?" I heard the word *essential* in my spirit. "What does that mean?" I said. So I immediately began to research the word and found out it means something that is vitally important, something absolutely necessary or indispensable. The Lord began to show me what was essential for me or anyone else to experience personal or corporate revival in their lives.

Repentance, forgiveness, unity, prayer, and *honor* are the essential elements of revival. These are the five necessary ingredients to living in and releasing the abundant life. All five of these elements are absolutely essential and are harmoniously connected and dependent upon one another. The Lord showed me the number five represented grace, and He gives grace to the humble (see James 4:6). It is His grace that empowers and enables us to live as more than conquerors within a world that desires to conquer us.

It is no surprise why the enemy is always attacking us in these five essential areas, because within these essential elements the expression of Christ is released unto the world. The enemy will do anything to hinder the flow of the Holy Spirit within our lives at all costs. Constantly bombarding us with offenses from our brothers and sisters in Christ that will eventually create space for bitterness to take root in our hearts. Humbling ourselves consistently every day and in every situation will empower us to live a life of repentance that keeps forgiveness flowing, unity established, prayer with the Father fresh, and honor as a way of life. It makes room for God to set up a stronghold within our interior world that cannot be shaken in any circumstance or situation we may encounter.

I will say revival is only a benefit when we make pursuing God essential instead of optional in our lives. When I began to make pursuing God essential in my life, He created a fire that burns 24/7 for Him. I am no longer living an inferior life, but I am walking in my true identity in Christ every day. Rivers of living water will truly pour out of you to create life and sustain life everywhere you go. Seeing lives transformed, shattered marriages restored, bodies healed of cancer and other diseases, chains of addiction severed forever, and people walking in a degree of freedom that only God can give is a result of what happens when rivers of living water are flowing freely out of us because we have humbled ourselves and allowed grace to empower us to live out what is essential for revival.

PASTOR MACK GLOVER
Discover Life Church
Panama City, Florida

42

The Song of the Ordinary Ones

History is marked by ordinary men and women. These ordinary ones suffered greatly under the iron hand of unthinkable evil or labored under the shadow of incomprehensible adversity. They were desperate like Hannah, Samuel's mother, who faithfully prayed until she received her promise (see 1 Sam. 1:9-18). She endured her pain until her promise manifested, and then she stewarded her promise until her progeny was birthed. These ordinary ones were often the least suspecting people of all for bold acts of courage or unswerving devotion to a cause greater than they. Their desperation postured their hearts to a place of encounter with the providence and the power of God. The coming global revival will be a grassroots movement of ordinary men and women who are believing God for a supernatural move of the Spirit.

The moorings of biblical relevancy have given way to a hyper-sensitive relativism. Many are crying out for God to reveal Himself in glory and power. Our nation has lost the security of foundational principles and the sails of fundamental disciplines that once held us at bay from crashing upon a distant shoal. Is the sound we are hearing the sonnet of a funeral dirge for biblical Christianity in America, or is it the song of the ordinary ones who are crying out for an unstoppable and sustainable revival in the nations? I propose it is the song of the latter that cannot be silenced.

The purposes of God are realized in the lives of such people whose faith and courage elevate them to a place of extraordinary sacrifice and fruitfulness. How many would know today that Martin Luther, the reformer, was once a sickly child living in abject poverty who would go door to door in his village singing for his breakfast? How many would know that D.L. Moody lost his father at a very early age and was raised in poverty by a disciplined mother widowed for over 50 years? In addition, he spoke with an impediment that surely would disqualify him from international fame as one of the great evangelists of all time. What about the unlikely heroes God used dramatically in their day to shake nations for the glory of God in great revival and awakening? These are ordinary people whom we may not have selected at all as being likely candidates for global impact. What is the story behind Wycliffe's intellect, Huss' devotion, Zinzendorf's missional heart, Wesley's strategy, Seymour's hunger, or Woodworth-Etter's preaching? These were not perfect people at all, but they were people God could trust and release into their lives the fire of revival and awakening. There are people such as these living in the earth today. The fire of God is being released upon their lives to carry the weight of God's glory today in global impact.

One of the things we must discover afresh is that one person responding in faith to a single impression or command from the Lord can unlock a myriad of events. This book, I believe, is the for the purpose of the unlocking of people and events that will impact communities and nations.

I was standing on the pier at Cape Henry. It was cold and raining with the wind cutting harshly across my face. I stood alone contemplating the past and the future moves of God. Suddenly, three ladies walked up behind me and one of them got my attention. As I turned toward her, she said, "We are intercessors from Maine. The Lord sent us here and told us we would meet a man here, and we were to give to him a message." She continued, "We believe you are that man. May we share with you the word?" I was anxious to hear what she had to say, and she continued, "The Lord says, 'The appeal has been heard, and the time of America's great awakening has come!'"

It was a simple but powerful word that we continue to steward today. God used these ladies mightily. My friend, you hold a key to unlock the promise of God for personal or even global revival. Are you ready to take your place in this revival and awakening of God?

RICK CURRY
Pastor/Revivalist
Rick Curry Ministries
Pensacola, Florida

43

The Rhythm of Revival

Awakening. Fire. Outpouring. These are a few words synonymous with *revival*. How about renewal. Stirring. Visitation. Maybe another word comes to your mind when you hear the word *revival*.

In the past, if someone would have asked me to describe revival, I would have used one of those words as well. It was only after genuine revival came to Christ Fellowship Church in Dawsonville, Georgia in February of 2018 that the Lord gave me another word to describe revival. That word was *rhythm*.

I didn't know much about rhythm. I knew it was required for music. I knew that it had something to do with proportion of sound, a distribution of beats, and that rhythm was vital in order to keep harmony and establish cohesiveness. *Rhythm* can also be defined as a measured flow. The Lord spoke to me and said, "Marty, I'm not so much concerned with what you call it as I am with My people getting in My flow and in harmony with Me."

Rhythm can be heard, yes, but it can also be seen. I saw rhythm for the first time in my life and it happened in the midst of the revival.

November 11, 2018—a day I'll never forget. It was Week 40 of the North Georgia Revival. God was visiting our church and touching people in our baptismal pool in an unprecedented way. We were seeing miracle after miracle, week after week in our baptismal waters. On this night, however, Week 40, several candidates had already entered the waters and had experienced a radical encounter with Jesus. Faith was high. God was moving in the waters. One after another they came. Then it happened. It was as if time stood still. I waited patiently for this particular young man to enter the water. I sensed rhythm was about to happen. Once he made it over to me in the pool, I took the microphone and began to ask him some questions:

1. What is your name?
2. Where are you from?
3. Why are you in the water?
4. Do you want to hold your nose?

Zach was a sharp, handsome young man who seemed to have taken life by the horns and was enjoying it to the full. He was calm and collected at first, but then he broke. Zach told his story of how he and his wife were facing divorce. His prayer that night in the water was that the Lord would completely restore his marriage. I prayed for him. Our team immersed him. As Zach tried to come up out of the water, his body went limp and lifeless. Our team of men held Zach as he "floated" on his back with his eyes closed for what seemed like an eternity. The Lord met Zach in the water and began to minister to him in a way no man would ever be able to. Did I mention it was Week 40?

Three weeks later, December 2, 2018, to my astonishment, guess who was back in the water? It was Zach! This time there was another stepping down into the water with him. Melissa, his wife, was coming to be baptized as well. Jesus had answered Zach's prayer and restored his marriage! They renewed their wedding vows in the water and were immersed together.

Ten months later, on October 7, 2019, Zach and Melissa welcomed Dawson Graham into the world. Dawson weighed 8 pounds, 4 ounces and measured 21 inches long. Rhythm can be seen.

Zach came to the revival and was immersed alone on Week 40. The number 40 represents a season of testing in the Bible.

- The Israelites wandered in the desert 40 years.
- Jesus was tempted 40 days and nights.
- A normal pregnancy lasts 40 weeks.
- Dawson was born ten months later (40 weeks).

Ten is the biblical number signifying obedience, responsibility, law, and completeness. Dawson was born on October 7 and weighed 8 pounds, 4 ounces and was 21 inches long.

- $7 + 8 = 15$
- $15 + 4 = 19$
- $19 + 21 = 40$

Zach came alone on Week 40, which just happened to be my birthday—11.11.18.

- 11+11=22
- 22+18=40

*Are you tired? Worn out? Burned out on religion? Come to me. Get away with me and you'll recover your life. I'll show you how to take a real rest. Walk with me and work with me—watch how I do it. Learn the unforced **rhythms** of grace. I won't lay anything heavy or ill-fitting on you. Keep company with me and you'll learn to live freely and lightly* (Matthew 11:28-30 MSG).

There is a *rhythm* of *revival*.

MARTY DARRACOTT
Executive pastor, Christ Fellowship Church
Dawsonville, Georgia

44

Moving Things in Heaven

We were three and a half years into our church plant when I decided to call it quits. We had sold out to do a parachute church plant in northeastern Atlanta, Georgia. We were convinced of God's calling and vision. We were all in for the risks of starting from scratch in a new territory with no contacts. But we had grown weary from the slow to no momentum. We had 104 people on opening day and had grown it to 82 people after 42 months.

So, I told a core of 20 people, "I'm going to come here to our rental space and pray every Wednesday night for an hour or two. We are bankrupt financially, emotionally, and spiritually. My leadership is failing and I'm not sure how to proceed. So, I hate to be a quitter, but at this point, it would take the voice of God to convince me otherwise."

We prayed for the next six to eight weeks. It seemed to me that God kindly whispered, "Make prayer the priority every Saturday and I'll show up on Sunday."

So, we began to gather in prayer on Saturday, and God began to move on Sunday. It was the season I learned how prayer moves things in Heaven to move things on earth. It reshaped the rest of my life. Our church had momentum from that day forward as long as we prayed on Saturday, which we have done relentlessly for nearly 30 years. Literally the only thing that changed our church was that we prayed on Saturday and we saw the power of God unleashed on Sunday.

This has always been the story of God. In Exodus 17 the Amalekites attacked the Israelites, so Moses sent Joshua to lead the men into battle. But Moses went up on the mountain overlooking the battlefield with hands up in prayer. This was personal for Moses. His livelihood, his family, the people, and his very life hung in the balance. But this was a real war. People were going to live or die. He had to wonder, "God, why do You want me on the mountain with hands up? What difference does that really make?" Still, Moses honored the prompt of God and went to the mountain. The battle raged as the Israelite men fought for their lives. And as Moses prayed with hands up before the Lord, he saw with his own eyes, "Israel is prevailing! Thank You, God. Whew, we are good to go." So, his hands got tired and he dropped them, no doubt grateful for the coming victory. But what happened next had to stun Moses. The momentum of the battle was now shifting in favor of the Amalekites.

In a rush of desperation Moses cried out, "Hold on, God, what are You doing?" And he began to pray with renewed fire in his soul. "O God, our mighty warrior, You freed us from Egypt, we are Your people, I beg of You—give us victory. Fight for us!" And no sooner did he reengage hands-up prayer but Israel gained the upper hand in the battle. In time, the confidence that God had given success settled in again and Moses rested his hands. And just as quickly Israel was losing again.

This had to be shocking beyond words. Hands up in prayer, we are winning. Hands down in prayer, we are losing! Moses now knew from experience—prayer moves things in Heaven to move things on earth! Sure, the whole world of humanity believed the real fight was being decided by physical warriors on the battlefield, but Moses had discovered the fight was being decided by prayer warriors overlooking the battlefield. Moses would never be the same again. So Aaron and Hur got on either side of Moses to hold his hands up steady for the duration of the war. Then the story closes in Exodus 17:13, "So Joshua overcame the Amalekite army with the sword" (NIV).

Did he? For in fact, Moses overcame the Amalekite army with prevailing hands-up prayer. And God told Moses to tell Joshua this story. I think it means that God wanted to make sure that Joshua knew the source of salvation to reinforce his very name change. See, previously his name was *Hosea*, which means "I am salvation"; but Moses changed his name to *Joshua*, which means "Jehovah is salvation." Joshua, in hearing his name, would have a constant reminder that the power that saves is God's alone. It is God's power and God's glory. This day was to seal the deal—Joshua, you fight battles with swords, but you win battles with hands-up prayer!

So here is God's invitation—get your hands up for your marriage. For your family. For your business. For the Kingdom of God through your life and local church. Get your hands up for your spiritually lost neighbors. Get your hands up for revival. For the Kingdom depends on prayer warriors to usher in the awakening. So will you rise up and become one of His hands-up warriors?

Kevin Myers
12Stone Church
Lawrenceville, Georgia

45

Whose Kingdom Is It Anyway?

IT'S DIFFICULT FOR US AS AMERICANS TO UNDERSTAND A KING or a kingdom because we were raised in a democratic society. Basically, we Americans question everything, we think for ourselves, and honestly we don't appreciate anyone telling us what to do. Conversely, those who were raised in a kingdom understand that a king is the sovereign authority and the people are subjects of the king.

It's been said that many preach the Gospel but not everyone preaches the Gospel that Jesus preached.

When Jesus began His ministry, these were His opening words, "Repent, for the Kingdom of Heaven is at hand." In our day, seldom if ever will you hear the word *repent* used in a sermon, and most of us have never heard a sermon on the Kingdom.

> *From that time Jesus began to preach and to say, "Repent, for the kingdom of heaven is at hand"* (Matthew 4:17).

The message of the Kingdom was the central theme of Jesus' ministry. It was so important that near the end of His ministry He instructed His disciples to continue preaching the Kingdom!

We Americans have more than most of the people in the world and in turn we worry more than the rest of the world. In only nineteen words, Jesus gives us the ultimate prescription to all worry and anxiety!

> *But seek first the kingdom of God and His righteousness, and all these things shall be added to you* (Matthew 6:33).

In Matthew 19, there was a rich young ruler who wanted to have the assurance of eternal salvation. This story in no way means that every wealthy person needs to sell all their possessions. However, in this case the young man's many possessions were the root of his problems. This is why Jesus told him to sell his possessions and give to the poor and he would have treasure in Heaven.

> *But when the young man heard that saying, he went away sorrowful, for he had great possessions. Then Jesus said to His disciples, "Assuredly, I say to you that it is hard for a rich man to enter the kingdom of heaven"* (Matthew 19:22-23).

Therefore, repentance is the key to both the Kingdom of God and the Kingdom of Heaven! The big question is this, for all of us who claim to be followers of Christ—if we are saved and headed for the Kingdom of Heaven, is the Kingdom of God actively working in our lives? Are we really Kingdom-minded?

We all know that we can be saved but at the same time be jealous and envious of others and how God is using them. Can we be saved and, yes, even Spirit filled but at the same time be solely concerned with building only "our kingdom" and not His Kingdom?

When a person is Kingdom-minded it changes the way they think about, relate to, and respond to others.

Characteristics of Kingdom-Minded People

- You know that prayer brings results, not just your own efforts.
- You are never in competition with other churches or church members.
- You are never in fear of losing what was given to you by God.
- You care about what God is doing every-where, not just in your area.
- You are not afraid of giving opportunity to others.
- You are not afraid that another church has more members than yours.
- You are not afraid of who gets the credit.
- You can rejoice with others when God uses them and blesses them.

As we see, the message that Jesus preached was that repentance leads us into His Kingdom. When we allow our focus to be His Kingdom and not our own, the most remarkable transformation begins to take place in our lives. The Kingdom of

God affects the way we look at others, relate to others, and respond to others.

The greatest question that we can ask ourselves is—if I'm part of the Kingdom, am I Kingdom-minded?

LARRY ROCQUIN
Pastor, St. James Community Church
Paulina, Louisiana

46

Are You Ready?

Then the kingdom of heaven shall be likened to ten virgins who took their lamps and went out to meet the bridegroom. Now five of them were wise, and five were foolish. Those who were foolish took their lamps and took no oil with them, but the wise took oil in their vessels with their lamps. But while the bridegroom was delayed, they all slumbered and slept.
—MATTHEW 25:1-5

I WATCH SOLDIERS WHO ARE JUST NOW ENTERING CHAPEL for services. They look weary, most have been up all night either on a mission or pulling guard duty. They bring their weapons with them and drop them on the floor, and then they lift their hands in worship. After service is over, they pick up their firearms and continue their mission. There is no respite in combat.

I want you to get this picture: soldiers never leave their weapons unattended, even in chapel services at Victory Base, Baghdad, Iraq. They have those weapons beside them just in case of an enemy attack. They are ready for combat at all times.

If we did that here in America, it would be a strange sight indeed, but not in a war zone, not in combat. The interesting thing to note is, we are at war in America!

What war, you ask?

There are dark spiritual forces at war with believers here in America and around the world. Make no mistake about it; we are in combat every day with the unseen enemy. Ephesians 6:12 tells us:

> *For our struggle is not against flesh and blood, but against the rulers, against the authorities, against the powers of this dark world and against the spiritual forces of evil in the heavenly realms* (NIV).

What do we need to do to combat the forces of darkness? Be ready and prepared! The Lord, in these last days, is preparing His army for spiritual hand-to-hand combat. Look at the parable of the ten virgins:

> *At that time the kingdom of heaven will be like ten virgins who took their lamps and went out to meet the bridegroom. Five of them were foolish and five were wise. The foolish ones took their lamps but did not take any oil with them. The wise ones, however, took oil in jars along with their lamps. The bridegroom was a long time in coming, and they all became drowsy and fell asleep* (Matthew 25:1-5 NIV).

The ten virgins' job was to provide light, and some of them, according to John Piper, had "lamps without oil, candles without wicks, torches without fire, light bulbs without electricity. They had the outward form of religion and no internal power. They liked their position; otherwise, they would have left. But they did not have a passion for using the necessary means to fulfill the point of their position."[1]

Five were ready, and five were not. Those five were distracted, too busy with politics or shopping or sports or whatever. They probably relished the excellent church services, loved the sermons, enjoyed fellowship feasts, and were very busy with the details of the day, yet the Bible tells us they were asleep! They were not ready for the coming of their Lord.

I want to share with you the secret of the US Army's success. The number-one priority is *readiness!* There is no other number-one priority. If the army was not adequately trained, equipped, manned, and supplied, what do you think would happen in the next conflict? We lose. Period.

The five virgins who were ready had oil, and they had their lamps; they prepared for the return of the groom. Are you ready? Here are some ways to start getting ready:

1. Take a good, hard look at your life right now. Are you focused and doing all that Christ has asked of you? How do you spend your time?

2. Start by repenting! Just start. When the army throws you into boot camp, on day one you are now a soldier, not a civilian. No looking back.

3. Determine to follow Christ every moment of every day by putting to death the flesh, that part of me that doesn't relate to Christ. In the army, you follow the orders of those who are

over you. Throw out all idols in your life—those things that are higher priority than God.

4. Fill your lamp with oil, which is the power of the Holy Spirit. We need power-packed disciples listening to Him every moment of every day.

5. Read and live the Word every day.

How shall we live in the now and beyond? Keep your weapons by you at all times.

David J. Giammona
US Army Chaplain, Colonel (Retired)
Victory Base Chapel, Baghdad, Iraq, 2005
Columbus, Georgia

Note

1. John Piper, "Jesus Christ, the Bridegroom, Past and Future," April 4, 2004, https://www.desiringgod.org/messages/jesus -christ-the-bridegroom-past-and-future.

47

What Are You Saying?

When Jesus came to the region of Caesarea Philippi, he asked his disciples, "Who do people say the Son of Man is?" They replied, "Some say John the Baptist; others say Elijah; and still others, Jeremiah or one of the prophets." "But what about you?" he asked. "Who do you say I am?" Simon Peter answered, "You are the Messiah, the Son of the living God." Jesus replied, "Blessed are you, Simon son of Jonah, for this was not revealed to you by flesh and blood, but by my Father in heaven. And I tell you that you are Peter, and on this rock I will build my church, and the gates of Hades will not overcome it. I will give you the keys of the kingdom of heaven; whatever you bind on earth will be bound in heaven, and whatever you loose on earth will be loosed in heaven." Then he ordered his disciples not to tell anyone that he was the Messiah.
—MATTHEW 16:13-20 NIV

CLOSE YOUR EYES AND PICTURE THIS MOMENT, AS IF YOU ARE there with Jesus and His closest crew. Can you see it? Can you hear the voice of our Savior? "What are people saying about Me? Who do they say I am?" Jesus then shifts to, "But what are *you guys* saying about Me?" And He's still asking this today! *Who do you say that I am?* Jesus is not on a glory binge here, and He is not concerned with His rankings. He knows for the Church to move forward and experience Heaven, we have to say the right things!

The power of life and death truly are in the tongue—every word we speak matters! When Peter gushes out, "You are the Messiah!" the atmosphere changes. Why? Because it was revelation! "For this was not revealed to you by flesh and blood, but by my Father in heaven" (Matt. 16:17 NIV). Revelation changes the course of our lives, and if we want to see the atmosphere around us changed, we need to be speaking whatever Heaven is speaking.

I want to challenge you to speak in three tones today in order to see your situation revived.

First, I want you to speak revelation in faith! Jesus responded to Peter as if what he had just spoken would change the course of all humanity. The entire tone of the moment changed when Peter blurted out that revelation. Why? Revelation spoken in faith! You need to pray and read until you have revelation for your situation and then speak the revelation you have with faith, knowing that what God revealed to you will come to pass!

Second, I want you to talk in *forward motion!* Apparently, everyone was busy looking back while Jesus walked through the cities of Israel—Elijah, John the Baptist, Jeremiah, all things of the past. Great moments, but past moments. Peter speaks of what is now and to come, "You are Messiah!" He is speaking in forward motion and I want you to do the same! Stop giving glory to what has happened and start speaking into existence what is coming. What is God going to do in your life, marriage, church? What do you see on the horizon? Let those things ahead come out of your mouth today in faith and God will begin to put them into place.

Third, I want you to talk in a *fixed* manner of speech! Your attitude should be—this thing is done. Jesus immediately began to speak in a fixed manner:

> *And I tell you that you are Peter, and on this rock I will build my church, and the gates of Hades will not overcome it. I will give you the keys of the kingdom of heaven; whatever you bind on earth will be bound in heaven, and whatever you loose on earth will be loosed in heaven* (Matthew 16:18-19 NIV).

What He said to Peter He will say to you in your situation today! *I will build. You will not be overcome. I will give.* Jesus began to speak in absolutes, and we should too!

Remember this today if you want to see your atmosphere revived. We are wind-driven and rudder-directed!

The wind of the Spirit drives us and the rudder of His Word directs us.

DEREK K. DRAUGHON
Pastor, Saraland First
Saraland, Alabama

48

The River Keeper

*In the last day, that great day of the feast, Jesus
stood and cried, saying, If any man thirst, let
him come unto me, and drink. He that believeth
on me, as the scripture hath said, out of his belly
shall flow rivers of living water—But this spake
he of the Spirit, which they that believe on him
should receive: for the Holy Ghost was not yet
given; because that Jesus was not yet glorified.*
—JOHN 7:37-39 37 KJV

ONE CANNOT SPEAK OF REVIVAL WITHOUT POINTING TO THE
Holy Spirit's work in us. He is the Reviver!

Revival is defined as "bringing to life again" or "a recovery of breath." Like a mighty river flowing out of its banks, it blasts away the debris that *hinder its flow* and catches up everything in its path.

Recently in a nearby state there was a contractor who dumped debris in one of their main rivers. The story was covered for several weeks on the nightly news. What stood out to me was there was a man who had charge of being "the river keeper."

The river keeper served notice to those responsible that they had so many days to clean it up. The state's fear was toxicity from the debris would contaminate the town's river, which in turn could spread disease and cause great harm.

Polluted rivers carry death to everything indigenous to it. In Ezekiel's vision of the river flowing out of the temple, it brought life to everything it touched (see Ezek. 47:9).

> *In the last day, that great day of the feast, Jesus stood and cried, saying, If any man thirst, let him come unto me, and drink. He that believeth on me, as the scripture hath said, out of his belly shall flow rivers of living water* (John 7:37-38 KJV).

The Holy Spirit *fills* us with rivers of living water to eradicate the darkness and bring life to dying world. If our river is contaminated with the debris of sin, it impedes and devalues what we are Spirit-filled for.

The life flowing out of our temple depends on how pure and unobstructed this river flows. The river flowing from God's throne in Revelation 22 was pure and full of life, clear as crystal. Revival is an unobstructed flow of God's power and presence carrying life everywhere it flows.

How is your river flowing? Is there any interference? Are you listening to the River Keeper as He convicts your heart for any defilement? Are you quick to forgive those who hurt you and repent of sin? Is your river producing life or death?

The Holy Spirit, our River Keeper, knows how to keep the river flowing.

As a small boy, I can remember my parents taking the trip to town to buy groceries. To me, the highlight was driving over the long bridge and passing by the dam just before you entered town. There was a small hydroelectric plant built on the dam, which powered much of the town. During storms, its gates had to be opened and closed to prevent damage from flooding.

Sometimes after a storm you could find all kinds of debris stuck at the gates and reducing the flow. But when the gates were opened wide it was quite a sight. The violence of the water blasted away the rubble, cleaning and freeing the way.

This is what revival does for us. We need to open our gates wide to Jesus and allow His Holy Spirit to flow through us, saving, cleansing, delivering, healing, and setting us free from all chaff.

Today, open wide the gates for the King to come through. If you long for revival, it is time to surrender to the River Keeper. Let the rivers of living water flow out of your spirit totally surrendered to Him. Let's pray this prayer together.

> *Father I repent today for my sin and all hinderances that I have allowed to stop the river of Your Spirit. Please forgive me, refresh me, restore me, revive me. Holy Spirit, make me so contagious I infect everyone around me for Your glory. Amen.*

David T. Coleman
Pastor, Harvest Worship Center
Stuart, Virginia

49

Swinging from Vine to Vine

Brethren, I count not myself to have apprehended:
but this one thing I do, forgetting those things which
are behind, and reaching forth unto those things
which are before, I press toward the mark for the
prize of the high calling of God in Christ Jesus.
—Philippians 3:13-14 KJV

Do you remember the famous story of Tarzan of the jungle? He seemed to have a sixth sense when he was in his element of the jungle. He called the animals and they listened. He lived with danger all around him and kept himself out of harm's way. He moved through the trees with "the greatest of ease," grabbing one vine and then the next, creating the image of flying through the jungle. His eyes looked for the next vine to catch in his right hand as he let go of the previous one in his left. Right then left as he flew through the jungle of danger with no fear. It was very noticeable how important it was for him to grab the next vine; and it was equally as noticeable how important it was for him to let go of the last vine so that he could move gracefully through this difficult environment. That was the life of Tarzan of the jungle.

I can't escape the analogy of Tarzan swinging through the jungle as compared to our day-to-day lives. Have you ever been stuck holding a vine, afraid to let go for fear of missing the next one? Maybe you find yourself in this place right now. You know—your life isn't going anywhere but instead you're looking at the same scenery each and every day.

What keeps you from moving forward? What has stopped your forward motion in life? Could it be that you have not let go of the previous vine so that you can grab the next one? Are you hanging on to an old vine that is not producing any fruit in your life, refusing to move forward and grab the opportunity that is right in front of you? Could fear be the enemy of the next opportunity?

As a farmer, I am interested in things that grow and progress in life. It is so beautiful to watch the transformation that a progressive life can bring. Life is very unpredictable and, at times, is not very user friendly. It seems to knock you down without offering any encouragement or acceptance.

How are you to make it? How can you possibly move forward? Let me make the following suggestion: *"Let go!"* Oh, I can hear you now: "I can't, for if I do, I will surely fall to the ground." Falling in life comes only from hanging on to the vine of the past. If you hang on like this, then your present becomes your past. You have the feeling of "just trying to hang on" instead of moving forward and feeling the wind of life in your face.

Flying through the jungle, as well as flying through life, comes from letting go of the vine of the past and grabbing hold of the next one in your future. You are to hang on, but only long enough to wait for the next one to appear. There may be times when you try to fly backward as you grab hold of the old vines of the past. You think you are noble in the remembrance of these past vines, and you think they will take you forward into your destiny. You are misunderstanding, though, that they have already served their purpose in moving you to where you are now. They have brought you to where you are, but they will not take you to where you are going.

Let's take hold of the wisdom given by the apostle Paul: "but this one thing I do, *forgetting* those things which are behind, and *reaching forth* unto those things which are before." This is the answer. Can you see it? This Scripture says you must "reach forth." You must leave before you can go, so *let go* and watch the hand of the Lord take you through this jungle called life.

ALAN SMITH
Author and speaker
Stony Point, North Carolina

50

What Is Revival?

MY HUSBAND, STEVE HILL, AND I HAD THE DEEP HONOR AND privilege of seeing the Lord move in such a powerful way in Pensacola, Florida during the Brownsville Revival. After we witnessed thousands of precious souls give their lives to Jesus Christ and hundreds dispersed all over the world to fulfill the Great Commission, I am often asked this one question, "What is revival?"

In order for me to truly express what I feel is "revival," I'll have to take you to Scripture:

> *Revive me according to Your lovingkindness, so that I may keep the testimony of Your mouth.* (Psalm 119:88).

David speaks of his own heart being revived in Psalm 119. He continually asks the Lord to revive him throughout the Psalms. Why is that? Because even David knew that we are always needing a personal revival in order to stay close to the heart of God.

So what is revival? I believe with all of my heart that revival is when each individual person is revived in their own heart. What does that look like? It looks like a lukewarm pastor who just lost half of his congregation through a devastating church split being touched by Holy Spirit and in turn his weary heart is revived and commissioned to preach the Gospel with passion and fervency! It looks like a rebellious son or daughter who has been addicted to drugs suddenly having an encounter with the one true living God and their heart is revived by His Spirit! It looks like a businessman whose heart has been cold from hearing the Gospel his entire life all of a sudden having a dream of Jesus dying for him on the Cross and his stone-cold heart is transformed into a revived heart of flesh! It looks like a grieving wife whose marriage seems to have fallen apart suddenly feeling peace from the Holy Spirit and her defeated heart is revived to intercede over her lost husband!

Revival is very simple—when Jesus touches hearts that are weary, rebellious, cold, defeated, desperate, and the list goes on and on, our lives are *revived* and ready to spread His glorious Gospel!

Steve and I were radically touched by Jesus in 1975 and we never looked back. Our spiritual hearts went from being bitter and hard to sensitive and filled with tears for the lost. Our favorite Scripture throughout the years has always been Psalm 126:6, "He who continually goes forth weeping, bearing seed for sowing, shall doubtless come again with rejoicing, bringing his sheaves with him."

If your heart is longing for revival, let's remind ourselves that weeping for the lost and continually spreading the beautiful Gospel of Jesus Christ will indeed bring in the harvest in Jesus' name! Let us also remember to follow David's example of needing a personal revival in our own hearts in order to stay close to the heart of God. That, my dear friend, is how we will see precious souls revived by the power of God!

Jeri Hill
President, Together in the Harvest/Steve Hill Ministries

51

No Sales on Sacrifice

*But King David replied to Araunah, "No,
I insist on paying the full price. I will not
take for the Lord what is yours, or sacrifice
a burnt offering that costs me nothing."*
—1 CHRONICLES 21:24 NIV

"FORGIVENESS IS FREE, BUT SALVATION IS EXPENSIVE. Salvation costs us our lives."

Hard to comprehend anyone refusing a free gift, especially a gift you desperately need, but David knew that he could not give something to God that cost him nothing. He had a detailed understanding that God does not accept gifts bought on a bargain, no sales on sacrifices, and absolutely no rebates on revival. The very definition of sacrifice is offering something that is precious. Therefore, if we are to place anything before God as an act of obedience, devotion, and worship, it must be the very best we have to offer. Having this revelation, we too understand that laying offerings before God will not be convenient and will not be cost effective, but truly sacrificial.

How could we believe otherwise? We stand before our heavenly Father who has spared no expense demonstrating

His love, devotion, and provision toward His children, even giving us His only begotten Son to cover the full cost of our expensive rebellion. Jesus actively illustrated His unmatched generosity through His lifestyle and by His death manifested the truth of there being no shortcuts to redemption. Our Savior exemplified this fact as He willingly gave us His everything, even to the last drop of His blood.

That is why I believe Jesus is found flipping tables over in the temple courts while stating, "My house will be called a house of prayer, but you have made it a den of robbers." People came as if they were shopping for their sacrifices. With money in hand, they begin bartering for sacrifices from the cheapest supplier, instead of searching for the best offering to present before their King. Once they haggled for the lowest price, they passed their transactional item over to the priest to offer to God on their behalf. No relationship, no care, nor much of any sincere concern, just a business arrangement between God and man. We have embraced the delusion that it is not our responsibility to pay the full price, but it falls under someone else's job description. We want the rewards but not the continued commitments. This is the lie that we have traded for the truth.

This was never God's intended plan, but instead His desire was for our sacrifice to be provided through our personal relationship with Him with consistent mutual interaction (see Ps. 51:16-17).

But that would be too steep of a price to pay for many. So we attempt to pave roads of convenience for people to draw near to God without paying the Psalm 24:3-4 price. We have taken away the cost of pursuit and the strain of the climb for mere convenience, and in doing so we have deceived ourselves with the false pretense that God is pleased by our intention instead of our obedience. This has produced an improper narrative of how we approach God and how we have access to Him. Week after week some of us as believers walk into buildings without ever having to pay a price to experience the deep things of God. We show up for services where everything has already been done for us. Congregations are then divided into two types of attenders—those who are after the things of God and those who after the presence of God. Those who are after the things of God could care less about His presence; they are solely interested in what He can give them, but those who are after the presence of God understand that He has already given them all things and now all they are after is *Him*.

That is why David spoke with such passion, *"No, I insist on paying the full price."* David knew the full price needed to be paid and no one else could pay that price for him. David knew his sacrifice was the entirety of his life.

Beloved, that must be our hearts' cry—all I want, all I need is *You, Lord!* Out of that cry we willingly lay our lives down as a living sacrifice to Him for all that He has done for us. This is the *call of revival* (see 2 Chron. 7:14).

Revival is not earned, it is purchased. It is purchased with desperate spirits and broken hearts that refuse to be comforted with anything else but this revival.

The question you must answer—are you willing to pay the full price?

JAYME MONTERA
International evangelist
Pueblo West, Colorado

52

S-T-R-E-T-C-H

TOWARD THE END OF 2019, I BEGAN TO PRAY FOR REVIVAL FOR myself and for my church. I feel as though I have always prayed for revival, but there was something different about this year. It was something that I'm not sure I could put into words, but it was just a knowing that this was from God.

At this point I did something that I have never done in ministry. I simply asked God if there was a word that He wanted to give me for 2020. I have had friends in ministry who do that every year and it seems like a good thing for them, but it just wasn't my thing. I'm not into catchy phrases and slogans. So I think it was actually a half-hearted asking of God. But to my surprise, to be honest, almost instantly a word dropped into my spirit. That word was *stretch*.

I remember immediately thinking, *Was that God or was that me?* I knew it was God but just didn't see the connection with anything headed into 2020. I asked God to please explain to me what this had to do with 2020 and even how it related to what I had been praying for, which was revival. The first thing I remember thinking was, *Is there a verse of Scripture with the word stretch in it?* My mind immediately went to Isaiah 54. It says:

*Enlarge the place of your tent, **stretch** your tent curtains wide, do not hold back; lengthen your cords, strengthen your stakes. For you will spread out to the right and to the left; your descendants will dispossess nations and settle in their desolate cities. Do not be afraid; you will not be put to shame. Do not fear disgrace; you will not be humiliated* (Isaiah 54:2-4 NIV).

It was then that I knew the picture God was speaking into my heart was more than what I was thinking. The above Scripture is talking about the future glory of Zion. In Scripture, Zion is often a type and symbol of the Church, so things started running through my mind. But there was more to the word *stretch* and revival than thinking about church growth. That is when God began to speak to my heart even more about this word *stretch*.

The Holy Spirit said this would be a year of stretching, not only for me as a person but for our church as well. It would be this stretching that would open the door for revival personally and for the Church. There are so many things that stretching does in the physical body that God showed me also happen in the Spirit. Stretching gives the body flexibility to maintain a range of motion. In order for revival, I know I have to be flexible to move with the Spirit. What happens to the body without stretching is that the muscles become shortened and tight. When that happens, when you call on the muscles for activity they are weak and unable to extend all the way. When that happens, it puts you at risk for pain, strains, and muscles damage.

The Lord simply told me that I will continue to miss what He is wanting to do because I simply could not extend myself to the point that He wanted me to go. To be honest, most people don't like to stretch, but they still want to experience the benefits of stretching. It is the same with revival. We want revival but we just don't want to be made uncomfortable through the process of stretching to see it happen.

It takes time to stretch so I can stay flexible and I have to continually make it a part of my life physically and spiritually. It must happen every day, and I must be committed to the process. I can desire to be flexible, I can pray to be flexible, but the only way to see it happen is to allow God to lead me to stretch because I never know when I will need to be flexible to see what God has in store for me and our church in this next season.

After all, Scripture says that in Him we live, we *move*, and have our being.

God, please keep stretching me!

TRACY HAMILTON
Lead pastor, Tri-County Worship Center
Seneca, South Carolina

53

An Unplanned Revival

HAVE YOU EVER ATTENDED A REVIVAL? MANY PASTORS, including me, have prayerfully scheduled revivals because we know the value in doing so, and there are many. In January of 2017, the church I pastor experienced an unplanned revival with eternal results.

I had agreed to host a local evangelist's annual four-day meeting for supporters and those who followed his ministry. What I did not know was God had a bigger plan in mind for Life Church Smyrna, which lasted for seven months.

We met frequently as we watched God perform miracles of healing and restoration for those who already attended our church and for guests who joined us. Many manifestations of the Holy Spirit, seen in the early days of the Church, were prevalent in our gatherings as the Lord confirmed His Word with signs and wonders. This revival was unplanned by man and yet it was one we had prayerfully anticipated for many, many years.

Amidst all that God did for others, one of the most notable miracles was the restoration of our own daughter. Summer Joy grew up in the church attending activities and being involved in every way. Even at an early age, Missy and I would say, "That girl could run most of our ministries!" Sadly, in her late teen years while attending Bible college, Summer Joy made some fateful decisions that led her down a very dark path for the next four and a half years. It was during those years that our family was torn apart and we sometimes wondered if we would ever be healed.

Our family prayed, fasted, planted seeds, and fought the devil because we knew Summer Joy's life was being attacked and she was unable to fight. Of all the promises from God's Word that we were standing on, the most precious is found in Isaiah 59:21, where God declares:

> "As for me, this is my covenant with them," says the Lord. "My Spirit, who is on you, will not depart from you, and my words that I have put in your mouth will always be on your lips, on the lips of your children and on the lips of their descendants— from this time on and forever," says the Lord (NIV).

We claimed that promise even when it looked like it may never come true for our family.

Summer Joy called my wife, Missy, on Friday, January 27, 2017 saying she would like to see us later that evening. Missy told her we were in revival so she would have to come by the church and to be prepared for the service to last for many hours! To our surprise, Summer Joy came to service along with her partner.

Without knowing she was our daughter or anything about her, the evangelist saw Summer Joy in the crowd and gave a word from God that was as accurate as if he had known her for all her life. Summer Joy and our family danced, shouted, and literally fell in the altar as we truly believed this was the miracle for which we had prayed for over four years!

Although everything did not change that night, the seeds for transformation were planted and the harvest would be gathered seven months later. It was on her 24th birthday, August 27, 2017, that Summer Joy came to church and ran to the altar at the close of my message where she surrendered her life to Jesus! She is now leading worship, directing our youth/young adult ministries, and completing her teaching degree as she follows Him passionately!

An unplanned revival? Not from God's perspective!

SHELL OSBON
Lead pastor, Life Church
Smyrna, Georgia

54

Revive Us to Be Revival

Then we will never abandon you again. Revive
us so we can call on your name once more.
—Psalm 80:18 NLT

THERE HAS TO BE MORE! MORE THAN WHAT WE HAVE SET-
tled for. More than what we have experienced. Why do we
feel like we are missing out and there is so much that we have
not yet attained? What is this longing and cry in the depths of
our being? We are in a search for a deep and transformational
encounter with our Savior and the one who gives us breath
and life. Job 33:4 says, "For the Spirit of God has made me,
and the breath of the Almighty gives me life" (NLT). We are
in desperate search for the life-giving breath that revives and
restores us to our original purpose. To give back the breath
in praise to the One who created us. We search for and long
for revival.

Oh, how we cry out for revival. But what is revival?
Webster's Dictionary describes revival as the act of being
revived—the act of being brought back to life again and restoration, to restore something to its original condition. It means

to restore interest in something again after a long period of no interest. Could it be that we have romanticized the idea of revival? In reality, our search for and pursuit of revival is, in fact, our admission that we have allowed our passion for God and the fire that once burned hot and bright to almost go out. We are called to be carriers of the very Spirit of God. We are called to be the spark that sets the world on fire and turns the world upside down. Our nation and our world are in a spiritual crisis right now, and we must reignite and restore our hearts back to a place where revival is not an elusive event, but rather a state of being. It's not something that we have the power to start or stop, but it is something that God does supernaturally in us.

We must ask ourselves—why are we *not* having revival? Why have we settled for less than true revival when we are called to carry revival fire in us at all times? I love what Leonard Ravenhill said: "The only reason we don't have revival is because we are willing to live without it." Are we willing to push past ourselves in order to see it? We need a true revival in our land, not just the emotional experience of great sermons and powerful worship. We don't need another visitation from the Holy Spirit but, rather, a habitation. We need a "move in with me, God" moment, where we say, "I want God to take up permanent residence in my heart and life and home."

Visitors only see the façade we put on, but if you reside in the same home, you see it all—the good, the bad, and the ugly—and it forces us to confront ourselves and change in God's presence. Personal revival will reignite the flame so you can become the revival your home and your community and your world are so desperately in search of.

We don't need another feel-good, comforting fire where people fall asleep in the presence of God. We need an all-consuming fire that burns away all that does not belong so that nothing stands between us and God. What separates us from those who have not yet been revived? In Exodus 34:29, the Bible tells us, "When Moses came down Mount Sinai carrying the two stone tablets inscribed with the terms of the covenant, he wasn't aware that his face had become radiant because he had spoken to the Lord" (NLT).

When God meets with us and revives us, then those around us won't recognize us and who we used to be. They will see the change and know we have been in God's presence. Our transformation will be the spark that sets our homes and our world ablaze for God once again for people to find peace and freedom and wholeness in Christ alone.

KAREN SCHATZLINE
Evangelist and author
Remnant Ministries International

55

Fire

IN RECENT YEARS, SO MANY CHRISTIANS FROM VARIOUS BACK-grounds and cultures are all sensing the same thing—the beginnings of true revival are occurring. It is common for all of us to hear, *"Revival is coming!"* Sometimes hearing that feels like a religious carrot on a stick out in front of the American church's nose. In spite of that, many are sensing that true revival has already begun, even if it has not yet fully manifest in America. It would be just like the Lord to humble the proud American Christian by releasing revival first in China, the Middle East, and Africa. Reports from our brothers and sisters in these places overseas are clear evidence of a purposeful, powerful move from Heaven. I would quickly add that I draw a distinction between the beginning of revival and the explosion of revival—we are not yet experiencing the explosion.

When that reality manifests, announcing it will be completely unnecessary. Nobody will be wondering if it is here or not.

> *Oh that you would rend the heavens and come down, that the mountains might quake at your presence—as when fire kindles brushwood and the fire causes water to boil—to make your name known to*

*your adversaries, and that the nations might trem-
ble at your presence! When you did awesome things
that we did not look for, you came down, the mountains quaked at your presence. From of old no one
has heard or perceived by the ear, no eye has seen
a God besides you, who acts for those who wait for
him* (Isaiah 64:1-4 ESV).

The Old Testament prophet Isaiah asked God to dramatically insert Himself into the midst of planet Earth in ways
that no human would be able to deny. *Rent heavens, quak-
ing mountains, spreading flame, boiling water*—what imagery
Isaiah used to describe the invasion of the Almighty! Even the
enemies of God will tremble as God moves in sovereign and
visible power. *Here is what is exciting*—rightly interpreted,
these verses have not been completely fulfilled. Isaiah's
prayer was not answered at the Incarnation, during the ministry of Jesus, nor upon the outpouring of the Holy Spirit at
Pentecost. None of those stunning historical events produced
the magnitude of visible results that Isaiah calls for in his
prophetic prayer.

It is my firm conviction that before Jesus Christ returns
to earth to establish His Kingdom, this planet will receive the
most potent manifestation of the presence and power of God
that has ever been offered. Yes, I believe that we will witness
mass repentance and salvation. Physical healings that paral-
lel what is recorded in the book of Acts will occur. Miraculous
signs and wonders will manifest that serve to prepare people
for the Second Coming of King Jesus.

How can I be confident that this is already beginning?

I see the establishing of precursors that must be in place for the Church to steward the coming awakening. *God is readying us to handle the fire.* There is purity that is being prioritized and pursued by Christians across the globe as we are hungering and thirsting for righteousness. Persecution against Christians is increasing, growing in intensity and frequency. Perhaps more conspicuous than anything is the increasing commitment to unity that is happening within the Church. Jesus' prayer to the Father in John 17 centered on one thing— glory for God that streams forth from the intentional oneness of the bride. Whereas Christians in the West have spent the better part of a century building walls between one another, we now see those walls being torn down and replaced with Kingdom bridges of unity that prioritize the fact that we are truly a forever-family in Christ. There is a generational hunger and thirst for spiritual oneness, which Jesus died in order to secure. What is happening right now is the swelling of a move from the Father, which is resulting in authentic, selfless, and organic New Testament oneness in the Church.

I will make you a promise—when the Second Coming of Jesus occurs, there will be zero denominations on planet Earth. Zero denominations.

There will only be the Church.

And she will be fiery.

JEFF LYLE
New Bridge Church
Lawrenceville, Georgia

56

Love

*Above all, love each other deeply, because
love covers over a multitude of sins.*
—1 PETER 4:8 NIV

THIS ONE SIMPLE VERSE IS PROBABLY THE KEY TO REALIZING true revival in your life. I know it was for me. When we learn this principle and then apply it to every relationship in our life, only then will God be able to use us to love those in our world.

You see, there are those who have done things or who are doing things that we know are wrong. They go against everything we believe, everything we stand for. We can point to specific chapter and verse that tell us it's wrong.

You're probably thinking of someone in your life right now. God has probably already been speaking to you about your relationship with this person, and for a very good reason. You've been asking God to bring revival, and this is where He wants to start.

Maybe you've had these thoughts: "If I show love or support to that person, will it mean that I support what they're doing? Will others who see me do this think I support that person's wrong choices? Will that person think that I am now compromising and accepting their choices? Won't this then destroy my witness for Christ?"

Those questions and more are all answered by First Peter 4:8. The word *love* in this verse is translated from the Greek word *agape*, which means God's love for humanity. It is a love that originated from God. It is a universal, unconditional love that transcends and persists regardless of circumstance. It goes beyond just the emotions to the extent of seeking the best for others.

This agape love that God is asking you to show toward others who are making choices that you don't agree with comes from a place that is outside of your origin. It comes from God! Remember the words of John 3:16: "For God so loved *the world*" (NIV). That includes everyone, folks. Not just the ones for whom you have an affinity.

And notice this—First Peter 4:8 begins, "Above all." This tells us that the other things God asks us to do are not unimportant. They do matter. But it *does* tell us that this one thing is the *most* important of His instructions. We are to love everyone with a love that comes from God (a heart that is willing to sacrifice His Son so that all may have forgiveness and abundant life); we are to recognize that showing this love is more important than anything else we've also been told to do, and we are to do it deeply.

Another translation puts it this way: "keep fervent in your love for one another" (NASB). Stay in touch. Regularly. Consistently. Be affirming of them with your words. Give them gifts of your time and your resources. Make certain that they know that you truly love them. Keep out anything in your words and interactions that might cause them to doubt your sincerity. Let God do the convicting that you think they need. Let God be the one to judge their wrong doings. You are to be the conduit of God's love, and His love is mighty indeed. A popular worship song these days describes it this way: "The overwhelming, never-ending, reckless love of God!"

God also gives us a promise in this verse. He says that when we do this, it will "cover over" the things we know are wrong. You may think to yourself, "Show love to them? I can hardly even stand to be around them." God says that when you show them His love, then He will transform you to not only be around them, but to truly be blessed for doing so.

By loving in this way, you're not endorsing anything that this other person is doing. You're doing what God is calling you to do, what God is empowering you to do, and then He is blessing you for doing it. When we love like this, the world changes for the better. This is how revival comes!

Make this confession today: "Lord, help me to love everyone always with Your agape love!"

PAUL WOODS
Associate pastor, Evangel World Prayer Center
Louisville, Kentucky

57

Is the Presence of the Lord Enough?

THIS QUESTION SEEMS TO HAVE AN OBVIOUS ANSWER. BUT IS it an easy answer? It is easy for me to say, "Yes Lord! You are enough!" Do I walk that out in my life? Do I prefer to know of God from a distance, or am I willing to enter the presence?

In Exodus 20, we see the picture of how the people only want to know God from a distance. Moses alone is willing to go deeper into the presence of God.

> *When the people heard the thunder and the loud blast of the ram's horn, and when they saw the flashes of lightning and the smoke billowing from the mountain, they stood at a distance, trembling with fear. And they said to Moses, "You speak to us, and we will listen. But don't let God speak directly to us, or we will die!" "Don't be afraid," Moses answered them, "for God has come in this way to test you, and so that your fear of him will keep you from sinning!"* **As the people stood in the distance, Moses approached the dark cloud where God was** (Exodus 20:18-21 NLT).

As I reflect on revival or renewal or hosting the Lord's presence or whatever label you want to use, its essence is how do I answer the question, "Is the presence of the Lord enough?" This current move of the Lord isn't a movement about filling stadiums or sanctuaries or swimming pools. It is a movement of Him filling us.

One of the harsh realities of moving into the presence of God is that most people prefer to stand in the distance. We must ask:

- Lord, do I want the comfort of the crowd more than Your presence?
- Lord, do I want the respect of the crowd more than Your presence?
- Lord, do I want the affirmation of the crowd more than Your presence?
- Lord, do I desire my sin more than Your presence?

Wait! What?

That's right. Moses pleaded with the people: "God has come in this way to test [prove] you, and so that your fear [reverence] of him *will keep you from sinning!*" (Exod. 20:20 NLT). Am I willing to risk having my greatest sin inclination destroyed by the presence of God? Pressing deeper into the presence of the Lord is actually hazardous to my sin.

How does this work? Every time I begin to approach the presence of the Lord, my mind soon has the same fear that the people had at Sinai. The same realization of Isaiah:

It's all over! I am doomed, for I am a sinful man. I have filthy lips, and I live among a people with filthy lips. Yet I have seen the King, the Lord of Heaven's Armies (Isaiah 6:5 NLT).

This is not the voice of God. This is the voice of man: "I need more fig leaves!"

As the Lord "proves" me, He removes my filth and presses deeper in me. As a matter of fact, it is His goodness that shows me my filth—not as a barrier to entering into His presence, but as an invitation: "Come closer! Let Me remove that from your life!"

He touched my lips with it and said, "See, this coal has touched your lips. Now your guilt is removed, and your sins are forgiven" (Isaiah 6:7 NLT).

My prayer for today:

Lord, may You truly be enough for me. May my comfort, my affirmation, my identity, and my purpose be found only in You. Yes, Lord, You are good, so I press into You. Take the coal, touch my lips. Yes, Lord, press into me. Holy Spirit, revive! Holy Spirit, renew! Holy Spirit, fill me! Have Your way in my life!

Jeff and Tammy McKneely
Pastors, House on the Rock Church
Amite, Louisiana
Southeast Louisiana Revival

58

Finding True Revival through Your Sufferings

That I may know Him and the power of His resurrection and the fellowship of His sufferings, being conformed to His death; in order that I may attain to the resurrection from the dead.
—PHILIPPIANS 3:10-11 NASB

I BEGAN FULL-TIME MINISTRY AT THE AGE OF 21. I BEGAN MY first journey as a senior pastor at the age of 33 in Kentucky. The church was called Calvary and it was at this church I would truly learn what it meant regarding "the fellowship of Christ's sufferings." I was eager and excited about this opportunity, while seeking revival and wanting something new for myself and my family. I had never really understood what that verse meant until I encountered suffering in church, from church people.

I attended the Brownsville Revival while serving on staff at a church in Mobile, Alabama. Our church experienced revival just before Brownsville exploded, but we would visit frequently. I was young and hungry for revival anywhere I could find it. So coming to Kentucky just a few short years later, I wanted to be a part of a great revival happening in the local church and community. I never knew pursuing Christ could lead to suffering and hurt in the church. I'm not saying this is the only way to revival, but true revival can be costly.

Flash forward to the North Georgia Revival. Once again serving as a pastor of a local church in the area, I was hungry for another move of God in my life and true revival. In 2003, I moved to our current pastorate and have been here since. I have seen good services and flashes of revival since being here, but none that were as sustaining as what we are in now at the North Georgia Revival. Revival has a way of revealing and exposing things—secret hurts, wounds, scars, and even secret sins. It also brings the opportunity to heal, forgive, be forgiven, and restore one's faith. It also gives a front-row view to miracles, signs, and wonders. Revival can be life-changing and impacting, especially for the wounded pastor/shepherd.

As a pastor who experienced great hurt and emotional scarring to both me and my family, it would take time to heal, but the greatest awakening moment to my being healed came while in search of revival. We all want *the power of His resurrection*, but we never realized it comes at the expense of experiencing *the fellowship of His sufferings*. So many pastors continue to do ministry while dealing with hidden hurts and wounds. Like Paul wrote, we think we are putting these things behind us while pressing onward (see Phil. 3:13). Yet the wounds are still there, unhealed, ignored, and pushed back out of sight and locked in our secret, you-won't-touch-me-again box.

Back to the North Georgia Revival. I have seen many pastors' hurts and wounds exposed, many get real with God in the altars and the water of baptism, but when pastors confront one another in love before the Body of Christ and ask for and offer forgiveness more than once, you know revival has come. It brought healing to me and my family, and it opened the door to understanding going through *the fellowship of His sufferings* His way. It truly opened the door to *His resurrection power* and so much more for all who have come and are still coming to the waters of healing and forgiveness.

Go ahead embrace the fellowship of His sufferings—resurrection power awaits for your own personal *revival*.

KEN GRIFFIS
Christ Cultural Center
Cumming, Georgia

59

What Is Stopping You from Commanding the Mountains to Move?

WHO DO YOU TRUST? SCIENTISTS? DOCTORS? SOCIAL MEDIA? The Greek pantheon? Billionaires?

God?

His Word says, "I will say of the Lord, He is my refuge and my fortress: my God; in him will I trust. Surely he shall deliver thee from the snare of the fowler, and from the noisome pestilence" (Psalm 91:2-3 KJV).

False beliefs reveal themselves in phrases like "trusted science" or "trusted officials" or "trust Hermes." Hermes, whose name is the basis of the word *hermeneutics*, is the imaginary Greek god of wealth, luck, and mischief. Jesus Christ, God in flesh, is the one righteous authority over every word in the Bible. Man-made beliefs (and religion) are prone to both successes and failures. God is both existence and eternity. His Word endures forever.

God alone is trustworthy. Christ alone.

When stock markets crash our finances or a pandemic shuts down our churches or the threat of global domination echoes in our news sources, we have the opportunity to walk by faith in Christ. But often we find fear in our hearts. We go silent. We risk nothing.

In an interview, Bishop Haitham Besmar (a former Muslim of 50 years whose physical and spiritual life was saved by a radical visit from Jesus Christ) told me, "Worry is atheism in disguise."

At this point you may wonder if you are somehow being incriminated. But God's Word says:

> *There is therefore now no condemnation to them which are in Christ Jesus, who walk not after the flesh, but after the Spirit. For the law of the Spirit of life in Christ Jesus hath made me free from the law of sin and death* (Romans 8:1-2 KJV).

Our Messiah came so that we "might have life, and that [we] might have it more abundantly" (John 10:10 KJV).

But How Do We Access the Power?

Before grammatical police alter my last sentence, consider:

Before there is light, *the power* of light must be present. Before there is love, *the power* of love must be present. Before creation is forged, *the power* of creation must be present. Before anything exists, God Almighty is the power. Dr. Michael Strevel made this point.

God is *the power* and we are called into a trust relationship with Him, but how do we get our quivering bags of flesh to surrender control and walk in radical obedience to Jesus?

While interviewing Pastor Andrew Wommack, a two-letter change in my understanding created a Holy Spirit flamethrower.

Of.

I'm paraphrasing, but Wommack effectively said, "You can't do it. You want to know why I have personally prayed and experienced the dead raised more than once? It is because I know it is not *my* faith that moves mountains. It is the faith *of* Jesus living in me that I do not doubt. It's His faith that I know can move any mountain that is within His will to move." Jesus said:

> For verily I say unto you, That whosoever shall say unto this mountain, Be thou removed, and be thou cast into the sea; and shall not doubt in his heart, but shall believe that those things which he saith shall come to pass; he shall have whatsoever he saith (Mark 11:23 KJV).

Jesus Is the Narrow Path

Does He live in you?

Does Jesus have *the power* to move any mountain?

Is the faith *of* Jesus enough?

In His strength, doubt vaporizes.

Asking in His faith must be done within *His will*; then, God promises you will receive.

Say this prayer now and act in the faith *of* Jesus living in you. Access both the Alpha of His power and the Omega of His will expressed in creation.

*I stand at the throne of God in Christ. In the faith **of** Jesus living in me, I **declare** that my mountains will now move. His power, living in me, leaves no doubt. I **proclaim** Your promises in Him **are** yes, and in Him amen. Abba, Your will be done.*

JEREMY T. LAMONT
Publisher, *GODSPEED* magazine
San Diego, California

60

How One Businessman Was the Catalyst for One of America's Greatest Revivals

Will You not revive us again, that Your
people may rejoice in You?.
—Psalm 85:6

In the 1850s, the city of New York and the nation were in a major spiritual decline. Churches were sliding downhill. Thousands of Americans were disillusioned with Christianity. William Miller, a New England farmer, had captured nationwide attention with his prediction that Christ would return on October 22, 1844. When nothing happened, many abandoned their faith.

The Panic of 1857 was a financial panic in the United States caused by the declining international economy and over-expansion of the domestic economy. Because of the interconnectedness of the world economy by the 1850s, the financial crisis that began in late 1857 was the first worldwide economic crisis.

Secular and religious conditions combined to bring about a crash. The third great panic in American history swept the speculative wealth away. Thousands of merchants were forced to the wall as banks failed and railroads went into bankruptcy. Factories were shut down and vast numbers thrown out of employment. New York City alone had 30,000 idle men. In October 1857, the hearts of people were thoroughly weaned from speculation and uncertain gain, while hunger and despair stared them in the face.

A quiet and zealous single man named Jeremiah Lanphier, who was a stock broker on Wall Street, of all places, was a member of a church two blocks from ground zero on Fulton Street. On July 1, 1857, Lanphier was appointed by the North Church of the Dutch Reformed denomination to begin a prayer meeting two blocks from ground zero.

Jeremiah Lanphier decided to invite others to join him in a noonday prayer meeting to be held on Wednesdays once a week. He distributed a simple flyer throughout the area announcing the prayer meeting.

At twelve noon, September 23, 1857, the door was opened and the faithful Lanphier took his seat to await the response to his invitation. Five minutes went by. No one appeared. The missionary paced the room in a conflict of fear and faith. Ten minutes elapsed. Still no one came. Fifteen minutes passed. Lanphier was yet alone. Twenty minutes, twenty-five, thirty, and then at 12:30 p.m. a step was heard on the stairs, and the first person appeared. Then another, and another, and another, until six people were present and the prayer meeting began. On the following Wednesday, October 7, there were forty intercessors.

Thus, in the first week of October 1857, it was decided to hold a meeting daily instead of weekly. Within six months, *ten thousand businessmen* were gathering daily for prayer in New York, and within two years, a million converts were added to the American churches.

Undoubtedly the greatest revival in New York's colorful history was sweeping the city, and it was of such an order to make the whole nation curious. There was no fanaticism, no hysteria—simply an incredible movement of the people to pray.

Hundreds of people who had always spent their nights in the gates of hell came to the prayer meetings that had begun in the evenings. Thousands forsook crime and became devoted follows of Christ. Crime and vice drastically declined. Wealthy people generously helped the poor whom they regarded as their brothers and sisters.

Ships coming into New York harbor came under the power of God's presence. On one ship a captain and thirty men were converted to Christ before the ship docked. Four sailors knelt for prayer down in the depths of the battleship *North Carolina* anchored in the harbor. They began to sing and their ungodly shipmates came running down to make fun, but the power of God gripped them and they humbly knelt in repentance.[1]

At the beginning of 1858, that Fulton Street prayer meeting had grown so much they were holding three simultaneous prayer meetings in the building and other prayer groups were starting in the city. By March, newspapers carried front-page reports of over 6,000 attending daily prayer meetings in New York, 6,000 attending them in Pittsburgh, and daily prayer meetings were held in Washington at five different times to accommodate the crowds.

Other cities followed the pattern. Soon a common midday sign on businesses read, "Will reopen at the close of the prayer meeting." By May, 50,000 of New York's 800,000 people were new converts. A newspaper reported that New England was profoundly changed by the revival and in several towns no unconverted adults could be found!

In 1858, a leading Methodist paper reported these features of the revival—few sermons were needed, laypeople witnessed, seekers flocked to the altar, nearly all seekers were blessed, experiences remained clear, converts had holy boldness, religion became a social topic, family altars were strengthened, testimony given nightly was abundant, and conversations were marked with seriousness.

Edwin Orr's research revealed that in 1858-59 a million Americans were converted in a population of thirty million and at least a million Christians were renewed, with lasting results in church attendances and moral reform in society.[2]

In the mid-2000s, Billy Graham proclaimed that he believed the next great move of God would be through believers in the workplace. Yes, Lord, may it be so!

Os HILLMAN
www.TodayGodIsFirst.com

Note

1. Adapted from J. Edwin Orr, *The Light of the Nations* (Bletchley, UK: Paternoster, 1965) 103-105.
2. Adapted from Bible Prayer Fellowship, P.O. Box 810718, Dallas, TX 75381

61

God's Final End-Time Plan Is Here!

And this gospel of the kingdom will be
preached in all the world as a witness to all
the nations, and then the end will come.
—Matthew 24:14

During a devotion time several years ago, I had a vision that changed my life. I saw the hand of the Lord come from Heaven and set up a series of six-foot-high dominos. The dominoes were covered by the glory of God. I asked the Lord, "What are these, Lord?" I heard the Spirit of God say, *"These are the 192 nations of the earth."* Then I saw the hand of the Lord return to Heaven. As I looked closer, I could see names of nations across the tops of the dominoes. The name on the first domino was *"the Philippines."* Then all of sudden as I looked, I saw the hand of God come back out of Heaven. This time the finger of God was extended, and the finger of God struck the first domino, and I heard, "Bam!" That domino struck the next domino, "Bam!" With consistent force, one domino hit the next domino so fast, "Bam, bam, bam!" until all 192 dominoes went down. I heard the Holy Spirit say, "This gospel of the kingdom will be preached in all the world as a witness to all the nations, *and then the end will come*" (Matt. 24:14).

This vision and verse changed my life and the course of our ministry. The Lord said, *"Contact all of your friends in ministry and tell them, 'Now is the time to believe Me for entire nations to be saved!'"* Until then, our ministry had done crusades in 275 different cities around the world. After this encounter, we had faith to take entire nations for Christ.

We called the first nationwide invasion Philippines4Jesus, and it would become proof that God's end-time plan had begun. Over two hundred international ministries joined the Philippine4Jesus initiative, and 310,000 Filipinos gave their lives to Christ during the 10-day campaign in 29 cities. We worked with 30,000 churches and ministries across the nation. In Manila, we rented the seven largest buildings, including the 30,000-seat Smart Araneta Coliseum, the 14,000-seat Cuneta Astrodome, and the 12,000-seat Ynares Sports Arena.

Coincidentally, the leaders of 21 nations of the free world (including President Obama from the US) were in Manila for a APEC summit, and because of the two meetings the president of the Philippines canceled work for a full week in a city of 29 million people! This allowed the people to attend the crusades across the city. Today, the Philippines is ablaze with the glory of God. Today, the nation is in full-blown revival!

Since then, we have done Ireland4Jesus, Bahamas4Jesus, and are currently working in Scotland, Greece, Swaziland, Ghana, Cuba, and Taiwan setting up nationwide events. We went into the 17 largest cities of Ireland and the 5 largest islands in the Bahamas with teams made up of 250 ministries and worked with over a thousand churches in each nation. We saw more than 25,000 salvations in the Bahamas. During our time in Ireland, a second historic event in downtown Dublin at the National Stadium was held where the churches of all denominations canceled their Sunday morning services and came for the City-Wide Pentecost Sunday I4J Celebration.

On Easter Sunday 2020, during the worldwide pandemic outbreak, I heard God say, *"I am pulling the trigger on My end-time prophesied revival, which will accelerate on Pentecost 2020 around the world!"* By the time you are reading this, we will have stepped into the greatest move of God since the book of Acts. These are the most exciting times to be alive. Everyone has a part in this end-time move of glory. Find a place to be involved. Connect and support ministries that are going into the nations. Ask God when and where He wants to send you, and pray for God's end-time plan to unfold.

God is in control of the last days, not the devil. Now is the time to activate your faith like never before. Faith comes not only by hearing but also by seeing. "We fix our eyes not on what is seen, but on what is unseen, since what is seen is temporary, but what is unseen is eternal" (2 Cor. 4:18 NIV).

Dr. James Horvath
Lead pastor, Calvary Lighthouse Church
Founder, W4J (World4Jesus)

62

Revival Glory: When Holy Spirit Paralyzes the Flesh

Or do you not know that your body is the temple of the Holy Spirit who is in you, whom you have from God, and you are not your own? For you were bought at a price; therefore glorify God in your body and in your spirit, which are God's.

—1 CORINTHIANS 6:19-20

IMAGINE THE REMARKABLY EXTRAORDINARY TRANSFORMA-tional moment in which the God who created you desires to peel back the heavens and invade the atmosphere of your life with His *revival glory!* The prerequisite for this divine encounter rests in the willingness of the blood-washed believer to position themselves to be a vessel of honor who allows Holy Spirit to consume their lives for His glory. Authentic *revival glory* is backed by the Word of God and requires a generation to be nothing less than the hands and feet of Jesus Christ in the earth. God is looking for a people who are fearlessly willing to recognize that they have the privilege and have been summoned by God to be a walking, living, and breathing advertisement of the Kingdom of Heaven!

God desires to cover the earth with *revival glory* until a generation becomes an eye witness and has firsthand knowledge of His great power in the earth. The battle lies internally in the daily life of the believer through warfare between the flesh and the Spirit. The Spirit of God desires to lay hold of your soul (mind, will, and emotions) and divinely influence it with supernatural power until your body is used as an instrument of righteousness reflecting the Word of God. On the other hand, your flesh (sinful nature) is at enmity with God and, fueled by the whispers of hell, seeks to wage war against the Spirit so that you do not do what God wills for your life. Refusing to ignore the daily warfare between the flesh and the Spirit demands the believer to die daily if they desire to become a carrier of *revival glory* in the earth. A spiritual fiery torch of revival awakening awaits the soul that will walk in the Spirit and not fulfill the lusts of the flesh.

I'll never forget one Sunday morning service when the *revival glory* of God came in and paralyzed my flesh. I voluntarily laid on my face before God during worship. While feeling the sudden weightiness of God's *revival glory* pressing upon me, I knew God was increasing inside of me. The heaviness of God began to weaken, paralyze, and fully restrict my natural body. The Spirit of God said to me, "Son, this last-day revival will be marked by My paralyzing power against man's way of doing ministry in the flesh!"

I knew the glory of God in that moment meant that the flesh of man would be paralyzed and the spirit of man would be mobilized at the coming of this great end-time revival. As I was pinned to the floor by the glory of God, I heard God's voice again, "Son, if you try to get off this floor again, it is rebellion!" My attempts to get up stopped at His voice! I learned that the cloud of God's glory *paralyzes the flesh* of man! I remember hearing someone say, "Pick up the pastor." They carried me to the people who were at the altar to pray for them. I tried to open my eyes, but because it involved the flesh they were sealed shut. I tried to move my arms and legs, but because it involved the flesh the movement was restricted. As I was being physically carried to the altar and my hands were placed on people's heads, they were shaking violently under the power of God's glory and I could hear the sound of immediate weeping and bodies falling to the ground. Though I could hear the sound of the effects of the Spirit of God, I was unable to see, move, or participate with my flesh in the release of God's *revival glory*.

I want to charge you to tap into a place of personal revival with God that begins with allowing Him to bring resistance to your flesh. In this place there is a fresh awakening of your spirit man to be alert, ready, and mobilized by the Spirit of God to fulfill His will in His strength as we are hidden within His *great revival glory!*

CALEB COOPER, D.B.S.
Author, *Pioneering Prophetic Patterns of Purpose* and
Jesus Focused: Awakening End-time Prophetic Strategy
Calebcooperministries.com
Pastor, New Hope Revival Church
Truth or Consequences, New Mexico

63

The Manifested Presence of God

He who has My commandments and keeps them, it is he who loves Me. And he who loves Me will be loved by My Father, and I will love him and manifest Myself to him.
—JOHN 14:21

THERE WAS A MIGHTY OUTPOURING OF THE HOLY SPIRIT IN the early 1970s at the church I now lead. Thousands were saved, delivered from demons, healed, and baptized in the Holy Spirit. Life-changing encounters with God were expected in every service. My family were members of the church, and this is where God called me into full-time ministry. The intensity of that initial outpouring dissipated after a few years, but the imprint Jesus made on my life and *the manifested presence of God* has remained. Revival for me represents an unabated and continually expanding version of what I just described.

Our church's mission statement is "Hosting His Presence, Equipping His Saints." Before adopting that statement, we took a survey to determine why people were drawn to become members of our particular church. This wasn't a multiple-choice test. The number-one thing people wrote was that they stayed because of the manifested presence of God, or words to that effect. Collectively, we place a high value on the Lord's manifested presence. I judge all Christian meetings by the intensity of His manifested presence.

Some don't understand the difference between the manifested presence of God and His omnipresence. The "omnipresence" of God means that He is everywhere at the same time (see Ps. 139). The "manifested presence" of God occurs when He allows Himself to be perceived. In other words, the Bible clearly teaches that Jesus is with us always (see Matt. 28:20), but not every Christian regularly perceives His presence. When we speak of His "manifested presence" we are talking about something personally experienced, beyond a theological truth.

Salvation involves a personal manifestation of our unseen Lord. The Lord condescends to make Himself known to us, bringing conviction of our sins and an awareness that we are in need of Jesus as our Savior. Every true salvation experience involves God manifesting Himself to a human being. This is glorious, but for many it represents their only legitimate encounter with the risen Lord Jesus. We dare not allow ourselves to become complacent, with salvation representing our only experience with the manifested presence of God.

For many years the Lord has very graciously blessed our church with His manifested presence and He's touched His people in assorted ways. This "touch" from God varies in intensity and people respond in various ways. There have been tears without limit, sometimes accompanied by great joy or even laughter. Many have felt heat (see Matt. 3:11); some experience something similar to electricity; others report feelings of being "drunk in the Spirit" or being temporarily overwhelmed and unable to stand (see Acts 2:15; 9:4). During intense times of prayer, many have smelled incense (see Ps. 141:2; Rev. 8:3). Others have seen visions of Jesus or visions of angels. I have personally experienced most of these manifestations over the years. I've also felt supernatural wind, seen visible smoke, and heard angelic voices singing in our main sanctuary (see Acts 2:17-19).

There is an insatiable, God-given hunger within mankind for His manifested presence. The devil tries to counterfeit spiritual experiences and he distorts perceptions during holy visitations of God. Every true disciple of Jesus Christ recognizes that there are sometimes excesses, and we must be vigilant to guard against them. However, in an attempt to guard against demonically inspired charlatans, we dare not negate the supernatural reality of biblical Christianity.

The Last Supper is the setting for John 14:21. Knowing that He was about to be crucified the next day, Jesus promised that He'd continue to "manifest" Himself to His followers. Jesus has never wavered from His decree, "I will love him and manifest Myself to him." He intends to have an unending, ever-deepening relationship with each of us. Demonstrations of His love are to be expected. Revival begins when our experience comes into agreement with His decree.

H. PITTS EVANS
Pastor, Whole Word Fellowship
Oakton, Virginia

64

Perspective

On the third day there was a wedding in Cana of Galilee, and the mother of Jesus was there. Now both Jesus and His disciples were invited to the wedding. And when they ran out of wine, the mother of Jesus said to Him, "They have no wine." Jesus said to her, "Woman, what does your concern have to do with Me? My hour has not yet come." His mother said to the servants, "Whatever He says to you, do it." Now there were set there six waterpots of stone, according to the manner of purification of the Jews, containing twenty or thirty gallons apiece. Jesus said to them, "Fill the waterpots with water." And they filled them up to the brim. And He said to them, "Draw some out now, and take it to the master of the feast." And they took it. When the master of the feast had tasted the water that was made wine, and did not know where it came from—but the servants who had drawn the water knew), the master of the feast called the bridegroom. And he said to him, "Every man at the beginning sets out the good wine, and when the guests have well drunk, then the inferior. You have kept the good wine until now!" This beginning of signs Jesus did in Cana of Galilee, and manifested His glory; and His disciples believed in Him.

—JOHN 2:1-11

HAVE YOU EVER LOOKED AT SOMETHING THAT OTHER PEOPLE are looking at and seen something completely different than what they see? For those of us who are married, it's almost a daily occurrence. I can look at an object with my limited perception and see something completely different than what my wife sees. We view things with different eyes. We have different perspectives based on our personalities and experiences.

There is, however, something uniquely available when I attempt to see the very same object from the perspective of someone else. My wife, who has tremendous creativity and artistic acumen, can see the heart of a created object and its reason for being. On the other hand, I am content with the fact that a table is just a table!

The more time I spend with my wife and the more dialogue we have around our perceptions, the more I actually begin to view things through the lens of her perspective. Well, at least I see a table for more than just a table, figuratively speaking. I can appreciate the beauty of a different perspective.

In John 2, the passage above presents us with a glimpse into what made Jesus such a polarizing figure. So much has been written and discussed regarding the prophetic significance of this story. However, the portion that grabbed my heart years ago is verse 11: "This beginning of signs Jesus did in Cana of Galilee, *and manifested His glory; and His disciples believed in Him.*" When I read this it jumped off the page to me. I immediately asked—what did the disciples really see that caused them to believe? What did it mean that "Jesus manifested His glory"?

I knew what *glory* meant, or at least I thought I did. In the Old Testament, *glory* meant the weighty presence of God, but I knew there was more—there was something that John was trying to tell us that was beyond a feeling that made these men give up their lives to follow Jesus. What was it?

The New Testament word for glory is *doxa*. *Thayer's Greek Lexicon* defines *doxa* as opinion, judgment, or view. This changed the way I saw this word forever and gave me a brand-new perspective.

What the disciples were able to see for the first time was the way that Jesus viewed a particular situation. He manifested His view or opinion of the situation. I have a conviction that Jesus never viewed the water as water; it was always wine to Him. The disciples had a front-row seat to watch Jesus address this important issue with a perspective and opinion that caused them to believe Him in a way that they had not to this point.

What Jesus did was prove that He does not see things the way that we see them. He showed us that a manifestation of His glory was the ability to view the same object that everyone else could see with a completely different and redemptive perspective.

We have the opportunity to inherit the perspective of the Man Jesus. We can move past the limitations of what we see with our natural eyes. Jesus has never seen defeat. He only sees dominion. He has never looked at cancer as something that could demonstrate power over His completed work on the cross. He has never looked at our deficiencies or humanity and concluded that our mishaps were too great to conquer the plans He has for us to give us a hope and future. He has never looked at our inability to "perform" and said, "I guess I missed it on this one." In fact, it's just the opposite. He has a totally different view and opinion of us. He is absolutely convinced that what He has begun in us He is able and faithful to complete!

By the way, when I choose to see things from another perspective, it opens my mind to the endless possibilities of what can be and silences the negative voice of what is not.

I challenge you today to position yourself to see things from Jesus' perspective—to view things from your position of being "seated" in heavenly places!

RYAN S. BAIN
Senior leader, Awakening Church
Louisville, Kentucky

65

18 Wheels and a Word

And when He had called His twelve disciples to
Him, He gave them power over unclean spirits,
to cast them out, and to heal all kinds of sickness
and all kinds of disease. These twelve Jesus sent
out and commanded them, saying: "Do not go into
the way of the Gentiles, and do not enter a city of
the Samaritans. But go rather to the lost sheep of
the house of Israel. And as you go, preach, saying,
'The kingdom of heaven is at hand.' Heal the sick,
cleanse the lepers, raise the dead, cast out demons.
Freely you have received, freely give. Provide neither
gold nor silver nor copper in your money belts, nor
bag for your journey, nor two tunics, nor sandals,
nor staffs; for a worker is worthy of his food."
—MATTHEW 10:1,5-10

YOU JUST NEVER KNOW WHEN A WORD FROM THE LORD IS
going to interrupt your day and set you on a new trajectory.
It happened to me on a normal day driving the short distance
home from a neighboring town. I do not remember where

I had been. I do not remember what day it was. What I do remember is the encounter that happened that day.

At the time, I was pastor of a small church in Texas. As I drove in the right lane, I approached a semi-truck and trailer. I quickly assessed the situation and saw that I had room to change lanes and pass the beast that was hogging the highway. As I moved closer to pass the truck, I noticed the phrase painted on the back doors of the trailer in very large print. If I remember correctly, the letters were red. (Hmmm…seems like I remember red letters being very significant.) Big red letters on the back of an eighteen-wheeler are hard to miss. The message that the Holy Spirit was about to release was even harder to miss.

The phrase staring at me from the back of this beast was this: "Presentation without demonstration is mere conversation." The atmosphere in my truck shifted as God began to speak. As I passed the truck, the message on the back became even clearer when I saw that this truck was carrying a load of vacuum cleaners. I recognized the brand and remembered an evening several years before when a vacuum cleaner salesman came to our home to try to sell us a vacuum cleaner. He told us about all of the features of this amazing machine. It was powerful. It was easy to use! It would clean like no other! Then he did the unthinkable—he asked permission to pour dirt on our carpet and demonstrate. Wow! When he was finished, the water in the vacuum looked like chocolate milk. He didn't just tell us what it would do, he showed us. While we did not buy the vacuum cleaner that day, we were impressed with its power.

As I passed the truck, the Holy Spirit began to speak to me. I had a heart for revival. I wanted to see God move in an unprecedented way. Something was standing in the way. I was going to have to embrace the truth that in order to share the Gospel of the Kingdom sufficiently, I was going to have to move beyond words into demonstrations of power. Revival would not come without embracing the "greater works than these you will do because I go to My Father." This stretched me because my denominational tradition championed verbal presentation as the vehicle to deliver the Gospel of the Kingdom without needing the displays of power modeled by Jesus and His apostles.

Speaking of Jesus and His apostles, look at what Jesus said when He sent them out on their first ministry assignment in Matthew 10. First, He imparted to them authority to cast out demons and to heal every sickness and disease. There would be no need for this if verbal presentation alone sufficiently presented the Kingdom. Second, He told them to declare that the Kingdom of God had arrived and was accessible now! Do you see it? Bold declarations backed by powerful demonstrations! It was the way of Jesus. It was the way of His disciples. He has not changed. His way has not changed. In order for His Kingdom to press into our churches and cities bringing authentic revival, there will have to be a recovery of demonstrations of power to go with our declarations.

Remember what the apostle Paul said in First Corinthians 4:19-20: "But I will come to you soon, if the Lord wills, and I will find out not the talk of these arrogant people but their power. For the kingdom of God does not consist in talk but in power" (ESV). The Kingdom of God is within you! The same power that raised Jesus from the dead dwells in you! The Kingdom of God is here now and is accessible! His power is not diminished! Declare! Demonstrate! Remember, presentation without demonstration is mere conversation.

CRAIG and SUANNE TONEY
Restoration Fire Ministries Center for
Revival and Transformation
Sulphur Springs, Texas
www.restorethefire.com

66

Nothing Else

They said to her, "Woman, why are you weeping?"
She said to them, "They have taken away my Lord,
and I do not know where they have laid him."
Having said this, she turned around and saw Jesus
standing, but she did not know that it was Jesus.
—JOHN 20:13-14 ESV

THE TORMENTING EMOTIONS THAT WERE RUNNING THROUGH
Mary and the disciples after Christ was crucified were overwhelming. For Mary, this was the man who cast seven demons
out of her, the man she followed, staked her life on, and someone she loved. The one she was willing to risk her life for
was now murdered, humiliated, and seemingly gone. All of
her dreams seemed to have vanished with the death of Jesus.
However, something inside of her said, "I just have to see Him
one more time." She courageously went to the grave and it was
empty. If the past 24 hours had not been horrific enough, she
now assumed someone had taken the body of her Lord and
Savior, meaning she was also stripped of saying her last good-
bye. The grief in her heart was unprecedented.

What she saw at the tomb would have been a climactic moment for many in Christendom and a supernatural encounter second to none. She saw not one but *two* angels in their glory and power. Not only was she having an open-eyed encounter with two angels right in front of her, she began to have an audible conversation with them. The conversation was straightforward:

> *They said to her, "Woman, why are you weeping?" She said to them, "They have taken away my Lord, and I do not know where they have laid him." Having said this, she turned around and saw Jesus standing, but she did not know that it was Jesus* (John 20:13-14 ESV).

Imagine the power and anointing she felt being in the presence of two angels. However, Mary did not seem moved by them or the atmosphere they brought. She just wanted to know where Jesus was. She never even let them answer her question before she ignored them to speak with someone she assumed to be a gardener. Wait a minute? Mary ignored two angels and didn't give them an opportunity to reply because she'd rather speak to a gardener, the man who pulls the weeds? That is exactly right. "Supposing him to be the gardener, she said to him, "Sir, if you have carried him away, tell me where you have laid him, and I will take him away" (John 20:15 ESV). She wanted Jesus, and nothing else would satisfy her. She had been in His presence and nothing else compared—not even a visitation from two angels in all of their majesty. Once you have been with Jesus, absolutely nothing else will satisfy.

Think about this. She ignored two angels for the chance that a gardener could tell her where His body was. She was hungry for Jesus in a heart-wrenching way. She wanted to know where Jesus' body was taken. John does not communicate that Jesus planned to reveal Himself to Mary first, or that it would take place at this time. However, Jesus could not resist. "Jesus said to her, 'Mary.' She turned and said to him in Aramaic, "Rabboni!" (John 20:16 ESV). Why? Her desperation unlocked an encounter. Her hunger created an atmosphere for Jesus to reveal Himself. Jesus witnessed a woman who turned down angels, and He could not resist showing her that it was Him.

When we get so hungry for Jesus that absolutely nothing else will do, not even angels or the miraculous, Jesus finds us to be irresistible. We must come to a place where we forget about everything around us. Where neither miracles nor angels will satisfy us above His presence. It is then we create an atmosphere and a runway for Jesus Himself to show up and reveal Himself.

> *God, I pray that You would make us so hungry for You that nothing else, nothing else will do but You. Not angels or miracles. As we hunger and thirst for You, fill us to overflow. Let us not be satisfied with angels and manifestations. Let us be satisfied with You and You alone.*

JOE ODEN
Author/Evangelist
www.joeodenministries.com

67

Heartburn

And they said to one another, "Did not our heart
burn within us while He talked with us on the
road, and while He opened the Scriptures to us?"
So they rose up that very hour and returned to
Jerusalem, and found the eleven and those who
were with them gathered together, saying, "The
Lord is risen indeed, and has appeared to Simon!"
—LUKE 24:32-34

TWO DISHEARTENED MEN WEARY FROM THEIR SEVEN-MILE
journey from Jerusalem stopped in the village of Emmaus for
the night. Unaware of the recent happenings in Jerusalem,
their newfound traveling companion set their *hearts aflame,*
opening the Scriptures to them. Urging Him to join them for
dinner, He did so, blessing and breaking the bread and van-
ishing before their very eyes! Jesus fulfilled His own prophecy,
split time, beat death, and arose from the dead! Who else has
accomplished this?

What will your heart do with this Man named Jesus? It
remains the question for all ages! Pilate asked this question

of the Jews and ordered His execution. Peter asked this question after His resurrection and went fishing. The people of Jerusalem asked this question and they repented.

> They were cut to the heart, and said to Peter and the rest of the apostles, "Men and brethren, what shall we do?" Then Peter said to them, "Repent, and let every one of you be baptized in the name of Jesus Christ for the remission of sins; and you shall receive the gift of the Holy Spirit" (Acts 2:37-38).

Are our actions any different today? We could disregard every warning as Pilate did, continuing in our sins, crucifying Jesus anew. We could busy ourselves like Peter, turning back to fishing. Or repentance is an option, as the people of Jerusalem did on Pentecost, turning their hearts toward God. May the obvious be our urgency! May our hearts *truly burn* for Him!

Peter's encounter in the Upper Room set his *heart ablaze*, preaching to the entire city in Acts 2. His example provides a clear four-step process for every believer's heart to burn for God:

Repent

The first step to refreshing is repentance. The way up is the way down! Humble and sincere pursuit of the Lord will bring spiritual refreshing and life, igniting the flames of passion for Jesus to every hungry heart!

True repentance is to turn away from sin and to dedicate oneself to the amendment of one's life. To change one's mind or course, to turn 180 degrees toward God.

> *If I had cherished* [not confessed] *sin in my heart, the Lord would not have listened* (Psalm 66:18 NIV).

The Lord Jesus is the same yesterday, today, and forever! He is ever rich in mercy, desiring fellowship with you!

Be Baptized

Philip's encounter with the eunuch of Ethiopia provides the second step for those pursuing, whose hearts burn with passion, desiring more of God:

> *Now as they went down the road, they came to some water. And the eunuch said, "See, here is water. What hinders me from being baptized?" Then Philip said, "If you believe with all your heart, you may." And he answered and said, "I believe that Jesus Christ is the Son of God." So he commanded the chariot to stand still. And both Philip and the eunuch went down into the water, and he baptized him* (Acts 8:36-38).

Water baptism is not a multiple-choice option to the believer; rather, it is an act of identification and obedience, making possible supernatural encounters of the God-kind!

Receive the Father's Promises

Peter revealed the third step, speaking of the promise of the Father available to every believer:

> For the **promise** is to you and to your children, and to all who are afar off, as many as the Lord our God will call (Acts 2:39).

Every promise is secured by request—*ask!* (See Luke 11:13.)

Preach the Gospel

Jesus Himself gave command to the fourth step declaring, "*Go* into all the world and preach the gospel to every creature" (Mark 16:15).

Peter set the example, obeying the post-resurrection command, preaching the Gospel with great power on Pentecost! The once fearful, discouraged, and bewildered heart of Peter was transformed into a *heart burning* for God!

The question for all ages still speaks—what will your heart do with this Man named Jesus?

THOMAS S. SCHAEFER
Lead Pastor, New Life Church
Bowling Green, Kentucky
www.newlifebg.com

68

What Makes Your Baby Jump?

WHAT MAKES YOUR BABY JUMP? IT'S A PHRASE TO ME THAT refers to the giftings, callings, dreams, and passion within the heart of every person who has a personal encounter with Jesus. It's a life-transforming moment that not only activates the passion to pursue Him but also accelerates the fire of the Holy Spirit to obey Him. Luke 1:39-45 says:

> At that time Mary got ready and hurried to a town in the hill country of Judea, where she entered Zechariah's home and greeted Elizabeth. When Elizabeth heard Mary's greeting, the baby leaped in her womb, and Elizabeth was filled with the Holy Spirit. In a loud voice she exclaimed: "Blessed are you among women, and blessed is the child you will bear! But why am I so favored, that the mother of my Lord should come to me? As soon as the sound of your greeting reached my ears, the baby in my womb leaped for joy. Blessed is she who has believed that the Lord would fulfill his promises to her!" (NIV)

There are times when people speak and nothing changes in your life. They may share with you about the weather or paint schemes for the living room. You try to listen, but your mind goes in a thousand directions. You hear the words, but they don't move you. Nothing changes.

Other times you are visited by someone whose presence changes the atmosphere. Mary had an encounter with an angel, and she had to share. When someone has a brush with Heaven, like Elizabeth, they begin to proclaim it to everyone they come in contact with. They tell about how God has saved, filled, healed, provided, or set them free. When they speak, the atmosphere around them changes. What they carry on the inside is speaking to what is on the inside of another. As the spirits agree, they are filled with the Holy Spirit and expect the Lord's promises to be fulfilled in their life.

Even though I grew up in church, I didn't understand the joy and fire others would talk about. I would see what God was doing for others. Friends would pray for me, but I became frustrated. I couldn't hear what God was saying, but I wanted to hear Him speak to me personally. I wanted to share with others the goodness of God. I wanted to feel my baby jump!

One evening, I was sitting in a room full of thousands of people who seemed to be having a holy encounter with a living God. I started thinking, "This isn't real. I can't do this. I am not good at faking." I reached down to grab my Bible and notes from under the pew to leave. I heard a still small voice speak, "Be careful not to judge what other people are receiving just because you don't. I know what they need, and what you need. Be careful not to judge the worship or their experience with Me." I broke at that moment and prayed, "God, I am hungry for You, but I don't know how." He replied, "Just keep pursuing Me." I've never stopped!

After someone has had an encounter with Heaven, like Elizabeth, they begin to proclaim it to everyone they come in contact with. When they speak, the atmosphere around them changes because what is on the inside is speaking to what you are carrying on the inside of you.

You listen as others get a word from the Lord but perceive that you are unqualified to hear His voice. All around you, there are people having powerful encounters, but you are still waiting for Him to visit you personally. When you take time to listen to His voice and obey, He will step into your life and breathe life where you feel dead. I encourage you—keep pursuing God. He wants to speak to you.

Ask the Lord to speak in a way your spirit is capable to hear. Watch for the birthing of a boldness to share what the Lord has done for you. Get ready, Jesus is about to make your baby jump!

DALE WRIGHT
Judah Church
Bristol, Tennessee
www.judahchurch.com

69

Passion Fuels Destiny

*To whom also he shewed himself alive after
his passion by many infallible proofs, being
seen of them forty days, and speaking of the
things pertaining to the kingdom of God.*
—Acts 1:3 KJV

It was in the spring of 1996 when I had an encounter with the Lord that would fuel my hunger and passion for revival. I had received Jesus into my life as Savior just eighteen months prior. This encounter happened one night while working second shift in an underground coal mine in western Kentucky, as I was operating a continuous miner (a type of machine used to dig out coal). Suddenly, I heard the voice of Holy Spirit instruct me to take a week off of work to go spend time alone with Him. I wrestled with this for the next 30 to 45 minutes because this was so illogical and contrary to common sense. The more I wrestled with this request, the more frustrated I became in my spirit, so finally I prayed, "Lord, this is the craziest thing I believe You have ever asked me to do! I can remember one time in Scripture that a hand appeared to a man and wrote a message on the wall. If this is truly You, then You are going to have to write me a message on the wall to confirm this."

Well, within the next 30 minutes as I was moving the continuous miner across the unit, I arrived on the other side of the section. On the black coal rib (wall) of the mine, someone had taken their finger and, in the white limestone dust on the rib, written the words, "King of kings, Lord of lords, Jesus is the way!" I had never seen that before or since in my 39-plus years of mining! As I read those words, I knew that I knew what I had to do.

The next morning, I called the mine superintendent and requested a meeting with him before I went underground that day. He agreed, and as I hung up the phone I prayed, "Lord, You know they don't allow people to take a week off from the mine, so all I know is You are going to have to make it happen." When I went into the superintendent's office that afternoon, I proceeded to tell him the whole story, but I prefaced it with the statement, "You're not going to believe this!"

To my surprise, after I told him I needed a week off to go seek the Lord, he looked at me and asked, "Well, when are you leaving?"

I responded very surprisedly, "What did you say?"

He repeated his question and I then stumbled over my words in astonishment as I told him I would be leaving that next Saturday. He then responded, "Be safe, I will see you when you get back!" God truly had prepared his heart as He totally overwhelmed mine.

So I drove over 250 miles and spent a week alone with the Lord with nothing but four gallons of water and my Bible. At the end of this time away, expecting some great revelation from the Lord, He asked me one simple question: "What's your passion?"

I responded with frustration, "Lord, I took a week off, drove over 250 miles, fasted, and sought You in isolation, and all You ask me is this?"

I received no response and was somewhat angered at the Lord for the next two weeks when suddenly I received this revelation: "One's passion is all that really matters because this is where one spends their time, talent, and treasure (money, possessions, etc.), which drives them into their destiny and develops their testimony!" Jesus' passion for the redemption of humanity, the restoration of His presence in and with us, is what drove Him to the Cross and kept Him there! So today, in quiet meditation, ask yourself in humble honesty, "What's my passion? Where do I spend my time, talent, and treasure? What is now, and what will be my testimony concerning Jesus and His Kingdom?" *Lord, help me to be all in! In Jesus' Name, amen!*

Tod Hill
Evangelist
King Fish Ministries
Madisonville, Kentucky

70

Breath of God

Jesus repeated his greeting, "Peace to you!" And
he told them, "Just as the Father has sent me, I'm
now sending you." Then, taking a deep breath, he
blew on them and said, "Receive the Holy Spirit."
—JOHN 20:21-22 TPT

GOD BREATHED ON ADAM AND HE BECAME A LIVING SOUL.
God breathed on the valley of dry bones and they were revived.
When God breathes on something, He is imparting His Holy
Spirit in order to bring life. Jesus told them as much when He
spoke to His disciples in John 10:10: "I have come to give you
everything in abundance, more than you expect—life in its
fullness until you overflow!" (TPT).

When Jesus breathed on His disciples, He was imparting
the very same breath that brought Adam to life, that parted
the Red Sea, and that revived those dry bones. He was imparting His Holy Spirit to them in order that they might become
His fully empowered ambassadors to the world around them.

That is the very definition of revival. That is the purpose
of revival. To fill us to such a point of overflow that we bring

life-giving water to a world that is desperately thirsty for something authentic and life changing.

The purpose of both personal and corporate revival is to usher the light of God into a dark situation and introduce His life where death has taken residence.

I am convinced we are missing the mark when we are simply "praying against" or "praying out" the darkness. When we do this, we are putting our emphasis on the wrong thing. We have the right intention, but in a way we're aiming at the wrong target. We need to move from pushing out the darkness to pulling in the light.

If we will simply pray in His light, the darkness will flee. It must. Why? When we pray in His light, we are calling Him to breathe on the situation, and His Holy Spirit resides where His breath is found.

God showed it to me in a simple illustration one day that I'll share with you here. Imagine a clear glass cylinder that is filled with darkness. As we pray in His presence, His presence begins to fill that cylinder from the top and begins pressing down on the darkness. As the light of His glory continues to press downward, the darkness is literally forced out until there is none left. The very presence of His light forcefully pushes the darkness out. It is impossible for them to co-exist in the same space. Where His light is, the darkness must flee.

What I just described there is the beginning of revival. When we bring His light in to push out the darkness, His presence, in and of itself, sparks revival. He heals that which was sick and restores that which was broken. The dead are brought to life. According to First John 4:18, He brings in His perfect love to drive out fear and hate. He introduces peace to dismantle strife and discord. His light demolishes the darkest shadows of sin and of death, and it illuminates the path He intends us to take on the way to achieving our created purpose.

God cannot be manipulated or forced to breathe on something. He breathes where He finds hungry hearts thirsting for the presence of God above all else. Hearts so removed from the cares of this world that nothing else matters. One only gets there when they are willing to lay aside their own pride and agenda in order to be fully submitted to Him and His will. Diligently seek Him in His Word. Seek Him through prayer and fasting. You will find Him. When you find Him, according to Proverbs 3:6, He will direct your path, and His path always leads us to revival. When you purpose in your heart for Him to direct your path, "Then you will find the healing refreshment your body and spirit long for" (Prov. 3:8 TPT).

That is the breath of God!

That is the key to revival!

ADAM REYNOLDS
Lead pastor, Assembly of Praise
Lula, Georgia
Love…Love…GO!

71

The Gaze of God

*But to this man will I look, even to him that is poor
and of a contrite spirit, and trembleth at my word.*
—Isaiah 66:2 KJV

THERE IS MUCH TO BE SOUGHT OUT IN THIS SIMPLE PASSAGE
of Scripture. To begin with, the word *look* in this text refers
to an intense look. It suggests one gazed upon, regarded with
pleasure, shown favor, and cared for.

How does one catch God's eye? Let's consider to whom
He will look. First, to the one who is humble. Henry Scougal,
author of *Life of God in the Soul of Man*, explained that "True
humility is not to think low of oneself, but to think rightly,
truthfully of oneself." Friend, if you want God to look at you,
get down off the "throne" and choose to become honest with
yourself. God gives grace to the humble.

Also, God will look to the one who is contrite of spirit. Are
you broken? The spirit of man here has to do with the center
or heart of man's personal activities—the source where his
actions derive their origin. The heart of man is the part that
makes you do what you do.

Oh, to know the fear of the Lord! God says He will look also to the one who trembles at His Word. Do you have an awesome respect for His Word? Are you extremely careful, hastily obeying what you learn? His Word is His advice, counsel, sayings, business, judgments. Proverbs 16:6 tells us that "by the fear of the Lord men depart from evil" (KJV).

A man's desperation for the things of God should melt away all preoccupations with self, notoriety, public image, and social status. Your hunger and thirst, if it is genuine, will drive you to eat and to drink regardless of the opinions of others. You will be willing to be a fool in the sight of others in order to be embraced in the arms of the Lord.

Have you felt the gaze of God lately? It is something you want to feel at all times. God has clearly set out the criteria for living. It is up to each of us to follow the pattern.

STEVE HILL
Evangelist, Pensacola Outpouring

About Todd Smith

Todd Smith and his wife, Karen, have served as the senior pastors of Christ Fellowship Church since 2009. Along with serving in pastoring roles for more than twenty-five years, he has preached the Gospel, led crusades, traveled to the missions fields, and participated in pastors' conferences in more than twenty-five countries around the world. He has also planted five churches in the United States.

Pastor Todd has authored six books: *Creating a Habitation for God's Glory, 40 Days, I Found the Secret, Word Power, He Sat Down, He Sent Him,* and *Speaking in Tongues: Your Secret Weapon.* He earned a Bachelor of Science degree from Samford University in Birmingham, Alabama, a Master of Divinity from Southwestern Baptist Theological Seminary, and a Doctor of Ministry from Faith Theological Seminary.

In his spare time Todd loves spending time with his boys, Ty and Ebo, hunting, and pulling hard for the Alabama Crimson Tide! Pastor Todd and Karen are currently traveling all across the nation and worldwide spreading revival fire wherever they minister.

For more resources visit www.kingdomready.tv.